CHASING DOWN THE ZOMBIE HUNTER

CHASING DOWN THE ZOMBIE HUNTER

THE TRUE STORY OF A SMALL-TOWN ACCOUNTANT, AN ELITE GROUP OF DETECTIVES, AND ARIZONA'S MOST TERRIFYING COLD CASE

TROY A. HILLMAN

PEGASUS CRIME

NEW YORK LONDON

CHASING DOWN THE ZOMBIE HUNTER

Pegasus Crime is an imprint of
Pegasus Books, Ltd.
148 West 37th Street, 13th Floor
New York, NY 10018

First Pegasus Books edition October 2025

Interior design by Maria Fernandez

Library of Congress Cataloging-in-Publication Data is available.

ISBN: 978-1-63936-967-6

10 9 8 7 6 5 4 3 2 1

Printed in the United States of America
Distributed by Simon & Schuster
www.pegasusbooks.com

This book is dedicated to my parents for loving, nurturing, and teaching me to harness the power of education and hard work. You are my foundation. Also, to my wife, for loving, supporting, and believing in me throughout this case and the writing of this book. You are my anchor. Finally, to my daughters, I love you more than words can express. Don't be afraid to blaze your own trail in life. You are my angels.

CONTENTS

A NOTE FROM THE AUTHOR

I never imagined myself, a small-town and slightly nerdy CPA, surrounded by blood, guts, and severed body parts on the hunt for the
most elusive of all criminals: the serial killer. For more than ten years,
I proudly served as a detective sergeant with the Phoenix Police Department in a very challenging cold case homicide assignment. During that
period, my elite group of detectives and I took down nearly one hundred
elusive murderers and gave delayed justice to the victims and their families.
However, the subject of this book, the three-and-a-half-year hunt for the
serial killer who savagely killed two women—Angela Brosso and Melanie
Bernas—in what became known as the canal murders was the most challenging and meaningful. The odds were completely stacked against us, and
the doubters were many. We were Angela and Melanie's absolute last hope
for justice, and we never gave up.

There were others who helped along the way, but the core group listed
in the following pages had the greatest impact. I would also be remiss if I
did not highlight a few strong leaders who, without their support, none of
this would have been possible. The original investigators were instrumental,
too. Without their hard work and diligence on the front end, we would
have not been able to put all this together.

Additionally, I would like the reader to know that police officers and
detectives are continually bombarded with graphic images of violent acts
and tragedy. Sometimes, the only coping mechanism or outlet for them

to remain sane is humor. The detectives on my team during this lengthy journey engaged in joking and banter among themselves. It was never meant to be disrespectful to those whom we ultimately served (the victims and their families). It is merely a coping mechanism for the human beings behind the badge.

CHAPTER 1
THE VICTIMS

On November 9, 1992, officers from the Phoenix Police Department made a gruesome discovery that upended a city for the next thirty years. A woman by the name of Angela Brosso had been reported missing the night before around midnight by her fiancé, Joe Krakowiecki.

Angela and Joe lived together on the third floor of Woodstone Apartments near Interstate 17 and Cactus Road in North Phoenix. Officers contacted Joe at that time but did not take a report due to Angela's status as an adult. Joe said that Angela went out for a bike ride around dusk on her purple Diamondback mountain bike, and she normally returned within a few hours. He told officers he stayed home and baked a cake for her twenty-second birthday which was the next day. When she didn't return, he and a friend went looking for her and walked the bike path she normally traveled. He also talked on the phone with her mother, who lived out of state. They found no trace of Angela. Joe told officers Angela was wearing a gray sweatshirt turned inside out, purple shorts and shirt, white tennis shoes, and socks when she left.

Around 6:30 A.M., he called back, and officers took a missing person report. That's when police started a search, and bike officers found a body that appeared to be Angela in the open field west of the bike path, south of Cactus Road, and east of the apartment complex. She was naked except for shoes and socks. Shockingly, her head was missing, she was badly mutilated, and it looked like the killer may have tried to cut her in half. A deep cut went all the way around her torso.

Investigators found multiple blood drops on the bike path. The drops continued for about 150 feet to a small tree just off the path. It appeared the victim had been on the ground near the tree and then was dragged into an open field toward the apartment complex. The body was then dragged more than one hundred feet up a steep berm to where she was found. Clothing was cut and strewn on the ground near her body.

Officers did not find Angela's bike, but they did find a bike reflector. Joe also said she always listened to a Walkman with headphones when she rode, but officers did not find the Walkman.

Angela's mother lived in Pennsylvania, where Angela was from. Angela had moved out to California a few years prior to attend DeVry. The summer before, she moved to Phoenix to live with Joe. Angela worked at a technology firm named Syntellect, Inc. as an instructor and had just returned from a business trip to Los Angeles the day she went missing. According to sources, she didn't drink or do drugs. Angela was known to be vibrant, athletic, and well rounded.

☙

Two days later investigators responded to the 11000 block of North 32nd Drive. This location was a couple of miles away from the crime scene. A retiree said that he had gone into his alley that morning and found some graffiti on a piece of plywood. The plywood had been there for several days. He had last been in the alley around 5 P.M. the day before and the graffiti wasn't there. The writing on the plywood read "I chopped that bitches head off." It was written in red lipstick, and officers found a broken stick of lipstick nearby.

☙

Approximately ten days after the murder, officers endured another grisly discovery. Angela's head was discovered floating in the canal west of Interstate 17 in North Phoenix near Dunlap Road. On the other side of the canal bank was a pedestrian tunnel that ran underneath the interstate, which was heavily traveled by pedestrians and bikers. The once vibrant Metrocenter mall sat close to the canal, a couple miles south of the area where Angela had been murdered.

An employee from a local store named BizMart called the gruesome discovery in to police. The employee told police a local transient and canal fisherman, Mark Qualls, had come into the store and told him of the sighting. Qualls took off and was nowhere to be seen along the canal banks. Qualls was tracked down by the police and claimed he had no involvement other than finding the head. A medical professional later opined he believed her head had been refrigerated or frozen by the killer.

᪐

Ten months later, on September 22, 1993, around 9 A.M., a jogger noticed blood drops on the bike path. The jogger then saw the body of a young girl floating in the canal. Patrol officers responded, contacted the jogger, secured the scene, and called the dive team. The team extracted a Caucasian female teenager from the canal. She was floating face up, wearing a turquoise one-piece swimsuit or bodysuit that zipped up the front. According to sources, the suit was extremely tight and appeared to be fitted for a much smaller person. The victim's breasts were exposed, and letters were carved into her chest and a cross below it. Like Angela, she still had her shoes and socks on.

The police discovered blood drops on the bike path near where her body was found in the canal. The drops appeared to travel about fifty feet and led to a large area of dried blood. It appeared the victim had lain there for a significant period of time. From the dried blood, there were drag marks that led into the landscaping just off of the bike path. The bloodstains went into a group of oleander bushes and a small tree. Officers found a bloody sleeve from a shirt, believed to be the victim's, and wires from headphones. It appeared the victim was dragged again down to the same bike path and then approximately one hundred feet past the entrance to the tunnel under the freeway. The victim was then dragged from that area of the bike path and placed into the canal. Investigators located what appeared to be her sports bra, cut and shredded, on the side of the freeway. Officers later found more items belonging to the victim in a credit union parking lot dumpster near the crime scene.

Officers discovered this victim to be a seventeen-year-old named Melanie Bernas, who was reported missing the night before. Her mother had left for a dinner, and when she returned Melanie was gone, along with her bike. They lived farther south of the scene, near 40th Street and Indian School Rd. According to her mother, Melanie rode daily, usually in the middle of the afternoon. She was last seen wearing a green shirt, blue shorts, white K-Swiss shoes, and white socks. She always rode a green Specialized Hardrock bike, but officers did not locate it at the scene. Melanie typically listened to a Walkman while biking. Officers did not find that, either—only the headphone wire.

Melanie was a junior at Arcadia High School and worked at a yogurt shop in the Arcadia area of Phoenix. Her friends and family described her as very responsible and pleasant to be around. She was not involved with drugs or alcohol. She had lots of friends and was described as athletic.

Either murder alone would have turned a community upside down. But now there were two, and evidence revealed they were related. The most heinous murders in the history of Arizona were connected to a single killer by DNA. The so-called Valley of the Sun was bloodied and stained forever by a fanatical serial killer. Fear blanketed the desert community for months and years, while the original investigators worked feverishly to track him down. Both cases went cold, detectives retired, and the public eventually forgot about the victims.

We did not.

CHAPTER 2
THE CPA

I made several abrupt shifts in the unforgiving plastic chair. I sat crammed shoulder-to-shoulder next to a host of other (I could only presume) equally uncomfortable people at the Illinois CPA Society. The walls and ceiling of the convention center squeezed in on me. Wave after wave of nerves thrashed, retreated momentarily, and thrashed again. I felt nauseous and peered around for the closest bathroom. The whole ceremony was a grand celebration for most, but I sat in sheer torment and prayed for my name to be called to inform me it was my turn to go up on stage. I tapped my right foot rhythmically to make time move faster. It didn't work. *Let's just get this ridiculous thing over with*, I thought.

How did I even get here? I remembered my obsessiveness for every single episode of the classic 1980s television cop shows: *Hill Street Blues, Hawaii Five-O, Miami Vice, Starsky and Hutch, Hunter, CHiPs, Cagney & Lacey*. It didn't really matter which one. I feasted on them all. The detective shows by far were my favorite, and I dreamed of the thrill of sifting through the clues and ultimately snaring the bad guy in the name of good versus evil, the cerebral game to outwit the scourge of society. It was my destiny, but there I sat. My destiny pointed bleakly to another course, one where I would jump with glee at the latest volume of governmental accounting or a new set of tax regulations.

Valedictorians from a small town were expected to make something of themselves. Becoming a lawyer or doctor fit the bill, but becoming a detective absolutely did not. I could work with doctor. After all, doctors questioned, followed clues of a sort, and ultimately solved the patient's problem. I was fully submerged in the acclaimed pre-med program at the University of Illinois, and it took me a nanosecond to come to a painful discovery: I did not like or even comprehend chemistry. That is, obviously, a massive problem for a physician.

There was my sign. I needed to promptly drop out and prepare to join the police department. The journey to become Detective Troy Hillman would become a blissful reality. I would strap on a gun and badge and follow my beloved 1980s detective heroes to make a difference. There was one problem: I just couldn't do it. I couldn't pull the proverbial trigger. I was still hung up on perceived expectations.

What next? I brooded. I had close family members in business. I also had an uncle in accounting. I was good with math. I needed a path, so I would give it a try. In a cruel twist, accounting came naturally to me. I liked the rigid organization and structure. For every debit there is a corresponding credit. I exceled at it and accelerated toward the degree and coveted CPA examination, a career that offered ironclad stability and a decent living. My detective dreams were shelved.

I drifted back to my current predicament, stuck at the ceremony. CPAs bear the burden of a certain nerd stereotype. The president of the society, who emceed the event, lived up to every bit of the stereotype. He wore the typical thick-lensed eyeglasses and spoke with a monotone voice. I imagined him brimming with excitement at the arrival of the latest and greatest set of annual tax updates or, even better, the updated volumes on governmental accounting standards. He would high-five his like-minded colleagues at the water cooler. I would prefer to hurl the monotonous items into a barrel and set flame. He said:

Ladies and gentlemen, there are three awards for the uniform certified public accountant examination taken in April of this year: the bronze, silver, and gold Medals. Each of these candidates about to be recognized scored, not only top in the State of Illinois, but top among 150 candidates in the entire United States. It is quite an achievement. Without further ado, the bronze medal for third place was a tie between twins. Can you believe that, folks, twins, getting the same exact score?

He chortled awkwardly, and I rolled my eyes.

"The silver medal for second place was also a tie," he continued. "No, it was not between triplets . . ." More embarrassing laughter. *Oh, for the love of God.* "And now, I'm proud to introduce this year's silver medal winners in the State of Illinois: Mr. Troy Hillman and Mr. Kyle Hood. Gentlemen, could you please come up on stage and join me?"

I wanted to sprint for the exit because I didn't belong here. These folks all embraced their *Revenge of the Nerds* stereotype. They had found their people. But I had not yet found mine. My silver medal counterpart, Kyle, was the only one remotely like me. I looked up to him as he was not only of superior intellect but charismatic, athletic, and adored by the ladies. However, even he had intentions to swiftly abandon accounting and launch into the fast-paced private equity world. *Was this my destiny?* I finally gathered the courage to step onstage and collect my plaque. Afterward, my parents hugged me with enormous pride and took what seemed like hundreds of photos. I faked a smile throughout while an inner conflict brewed.

Friends and family barraged me with "With that score, you're partner material, Troy." *Partner material, partner material, partner material* looped incessantly in my mind. The torment would not stop.

❧

The necktie had an iron chokehold, and the wool suitcoat engulfed me in sweat. I sat in a musty board room at a museum and meticulously wrote numbers in an accounting ledger. I added column after column of numbers together. The numbers were extracted painstakingly from last year's cash flow statement. I wondered if anyone anywhere cared about last year's cash flow statement. Calculators clicked and clattered in the background. I checked my watch and realized it was only one o'clock in the afternoon. I shuddered at another seven or more hours to go. *An eternity.*

I glanced down at the police manual tucked in my audit bag. The manual was a step-by-step guide on how to test and land a position with a police department. I carried it to remind me that I had a choice. I would occasionally reach down and touch it. It radiated power and control.

My manager walked by and focused intently on my cash flow statement. I drove back my blossoming urge. I wanted to wad up the numbers nobody cared about and hurl it toward him, to scream that someone else could do this boring and unfulfilling job. I desired a permanent escape from the mundane museum and the accounting chains that held me. I wanted nothing more than to yell proudly that I am off to become Sherlock Holmes and make a difference.

My fantasy fled. The manager told me that we would be staying late again. I felt like an inmate trapped in a prison the likes of Alcatraz. Yet, unlike that nightmare, I had the key. I had a way out, if I would only listen to my gut. *If only.*

I lingered alone in the elevator for what seemed to be an eternity. I stared at the long column of buttons. I needed to hit the button for the thirtieth floor, but my hand shook. I pulled it away multiple times at the very moment I was about to tap it. I was facing my destiny. Sweat beads ran down my back in my stifling business suit. I tugged at my ironlike necktie while my heart pounded in my chest. I had a crushing headache and felt woozy. *Just hit the stupid button, Hillman. This must be done. You were ordered to see him.* The elevator moaned. I took long breaths to soothe my angst on the longest ride imaginable.

When the doors slammed behind me, I smelled the faint scent of cinnamon. I tried to focus on that comforting smell, but it didn't work. Down the hallway toward the receptionist's desk, I saw the fire escape stairwell. *That's it! I would escape.* The receptionist called out, "You must be Troy."

Despite more and more back sweat and a throttled heart rate, I said, "Yes, ma'am."

"You can go in. He's expecting you."

I crept into the managing partner's office of one of the largest accounting firms in the world. I wished I could just slide him a note that read "I quit" and run off without further explanation. That would be too easy. His massive office, lined with wall-to-wall mahogany wood, looked down on most of the towering Chicago skyline. It was breathtaking. In any other situation, I would have been overjoyed to take it all in. The partner stared out the window toward Lake Michigan with his back toward me. *I could just leap past him and throw myself out the window,* I thought. That didn't help.

I cleared my throat. "Sir, you wanted to see me?"

The partner stood up. He was a tall, distinguished, intimidating man who wore $2,000 suits and drove the latest and greatest Porsche. I was a delicate mess of a young man about to turn his back on a lucrative career and chase a dream I knew little about. My knees buckled and the sweat spread in an all-out formation from my back to my brow. I was a steamy mess.

"Yes, Troy, come on in. I don't think that we've met before, but I wanted to meet with you directly. I understand that you've submitted your resignation, and frankly, I am a bit concerned. The HR director tells me that you had extremely good grades at the University of Illinois and scored extremely high on the CPA exam. I've heard nothing but good things during your tenure with our firm. I'm told that you are becoming a . . . police officer? Is that correct, young man?" He looked at me through his thick glasses with a deep frown.

I took a deep breath, summoned my inner strength, and said, "Yes, sir. Phoenix PD. I want to be a detective." Even though I teetered on the edge of cardiac arrest, a wave of relief held me. I had said what I needed to say.

He blew out a deep sigh. "Troy, a guy like you could make partner rather quickly. You have a great life ahead of you with this firm and in the business world. I've been afforded the best of cars, suits, and vacations. So, I'll just come out and say it: We've never had a member of our staff quit to become a cop. Ever." He pulled off his thick glasses and looked at me. "I mean, seriously?"

"Well, sir, consider me the first to become a lowly cop and future lowly detective. I appreciate your kind words and concern. However, I stand by my decision. Good day, sir." He stood behind his desk, staring blankly at me as I walked out of the office. I didn't look back.

The year 1997 was a tipping point in my life.

CHAPTER 3
THE CANAL MURDERS DISSECTED

The room was nothing special, but it would do. It consisted of a simple collection of wooden tables and a few scattered metal folding chairs. More importantly, every wall in the large room had either a big bulletin or dry erase board. I, like most detectives, am a visual creature, and I needed to gaze at every detail of these murders. Among those details was the key, I knew, to finding the killer. It was the classic find-the-hidden-object-in-the-picture game I loved as a child. Only this was no game. Even though I turned my back on the CPA profession years ago, the methodology used to flush out why the debits did not equal the credits was still hardwired inside of me. A CPA's extreme organization and obsession with every detail would prove effective—I believed this. By the time I had gotten access to the case files, almost twenty years had passed since Angela's and Melanie's murders, and they deserved justice.

I graduated from the police academy in 1998 and launched into patrolling the streets of South Phoenix followed by a stint as a financial crimes detective and onto a patrol sergeant/squad leader. The original case agent for the canal murders was thorough and diligent but retired in 1997. The case had been handed over to the scene agent who worked on it as time permitted. However, as Phoenix grew in the late 1990s and early 2000s, so did the murder rate. Homicide detectives were swamped with new cases and had little time for cold cases. Even when cold case detectives were added to the mix in the mid-2000s to help, they didn't have time to review thousands of cases.

The perpetrator's DNA profile for the canal murders was uploaded into the national DNA database in the late 1990s, and there were no hits. Time marched on. The canal murders investigation and files were absolutely massive, and I can only imagine it was easier to assume and hope that the perpetrator was dead or at the very least causing destruction in other parts of the country.

My obsession with these two cases, the canal murders, began a few weeks earlier when I received a media-generated public records request. To protect the victims and their investigations, I would spend innumerable eye-straining hours poring line by line through materials for every public records request, redacting it painstakingly. I wanted to ensure that sensitive information did not get out, should the case eventually go to trial. *We owed that much to the victims and their families*, I thought. These reports were different, though. Not only were they massive, using reams and reams of paper, but they reeked of a serial killer. The acts committed upon these two women were beyond savage. It was something reserved for Hollywood, and I doubted even the most twisted script writers could come up with what I was seeing. My heart ached with each turn of the page. Many of the salty homicide investigators at the time adamantly stated the killer was dead. Yet, even if this were the case, I believed there had to have been more murders before and after. One didn't start out with beheading a human being and mutilating a corpse and move on to post-mortem acts of carving and re-dressing, like the second murder, and then just stop. There had to be more despicable and predatory behavior both before and after. I could and would not accept the notion he was dead.

I took a photograph of our first victim, Angela Brosso, and taped it to the whiteboard. I stared sorrowfully at the photo. Angela was an intelligent, beautiful, and vibrant blond woman with her whole life in front of her. She had grown up in a small town in Pennsylvania and pursued her dreams of an IT career by moving to Los Angeles to attend DeVry and then on to Phoenix. Angela was newly engaged to a man she had met at a college campus in New Jersey named Joe Krakowiecki, and they lived together in an apartment adjacent to where her body was found. Her last bike ride took place on the eve of her twenty-second birthday. She had just returned from a trip to Los Angeles as a trainer for her employer, Syntellect, Inc. I glumly jotted down these notes underneath the photo and put "Victim #1—November 1992" above her picture.

I posted a photo of Angela's fiancé, Joe, a few feet away from Angela's and drew a connection arrow, labeling it "fiancé/last person to see her alive." Joe was considered the prime suspect during the initial stages of the investigation and had been interviewed three separate times. Joe told investigators he met Angela at DeVry in New Jersey in April 1991. In October 1991, Angela moved to California and completed her degree, whereas he went to Phoenix to continue his DeVry education. Angela moved in with him at the apartment Joe had at the time after graduating the summer of 1992. Joe said they had very good relationship with only small fights.

According to Joe, Angela had gone on teaching assignment to Los Angeles and returned the day prior after midnight. They slept until 11 A.M. on Sunday and went to pick up her bike around noon. They ate at TGI Friday's restaurant, ran to the grocery store, and were home by 7 P.M. Angela went for her bike ride around dusk, but Joe didn't go with her because he wanted to bake her a birthday cake. Angela was usually gone for forty-five minutes on a ride. Joe said he looked for her on three occasions that night and called the police.

Detectives focused on Joe not only because he was the last person to see Angela alive but due to concerning statements from her mother about Joe's behavior and their relationship. Angela's mother said Joe acted strangely when she called him multiple times on the night Angela went missing. Joe did not seem worried or concerned. Angela's mother told Joe to check the bike path, but he said he and a friend had checked the bike path multiple times. Angela's mother said Joe and Angela had been having problems for the past three weeks and Angela was going to move back to Pennsylvania but needed money. She added that Joe was not supportive of Angela's teaching job and was drinking and partying a lot. Angela had told her mother that Joe had pushed her in the past.

Coworkers of Angela added to Angela's mother's statements. They all said she wanted to move out due to problems with Joe. Joe maintained his innocence throughout. There was also no known connection to the second victim, Melanie. Joe was ruled out as a suspect in the mid-1990s by DNA comparison to the DNA left at the scene by the perpetrator. I wrote notes under Joe and indicated "ruled out by DNA."

I took another gulp of coffee and plowed back into the case. I taped a photo of the second victim, Melanie Bernas, a few feet away from Angela's. I wrote "Victim #2—September 1993" above Melanie's photo and drew a connection line. The same feelings of sadness overwhelmed me as with Angela. Melanie was even younger than Angela, at seventeen, just a high school junior. I sighed and rubbed my temple. Melanie was likewise intelligent and beautiful with a full life ahead of her. Investigators spoke with Melanie's mother and her friends. According to Melanie's mother, she had last seen Melanie at their home at about 7 P.M. when she left to go out to dinner. When Melanie's mother returned home around 10 P.M., Melanie was not there, and her bike was gone. In the past, Melanie rode her bike for exercise and rode city bike paths northwest of their home to Metrocenter, which was in North Central Phoenix. Melanie must have gone out sometime after her mother left. Her mother reported Melanie missing the next morning.

Melanie's close friends told investigators she didn't use drugs but did drink occasionally. Melanie did not have a boyfriend. Her best friend went over to Melanie's house on the night she went missing at 8:10 P.M. At the time, the doors were locked, and Melanie's bike was gone. I wrote these notes underneath Melanie's photo.

I gazed at the three photos, Angela, Melanie, and Joe. I felt I had made some progress, but I was still lost and melancholy. I posted a photo of a man named Mark Qualls near Angela and Joe. The killer had taken Angela's head from the scene, and approximately ten days later it was found floating in the canal. Qualls was a local transient and canal fisherman. Qualls had told an employee of a store to call police and took off. Interestingly, Qualls was nicknamed the Fisher King. Detectives tracked the Fisher King down to a local bar. He was interviewed and said he had been there the night before fishing until dusk. At that time, there was no head there. He walked by the canal in the morning and saw it. Qualls adamantly denied involvement and gave a blood sample.

I drew a squiggly line from Qualls to Angela and wrote "found her head." I jotted down notes below Qualls's photo. I also drew a crude representation of a letter connecting it to Angela. I wrote, "letter from the doctor in D.C. on how long Angela's head was in the canal. The doctor's working theory was that the perpetrator preserved the head through refrigeration or freezing." *Dreadful*, I thought. *Absolutely dreadful.*

On a separate whiteboard to the left of the victim's photos, I detailed the location of each murder drawing a crude map labeled "ONE—Angela's murder (1992), TWO—Melanie's murder (1993)." Eerily, Angela's head was found very close to where Melanie was later found murdered. It was just on the other side of a major freeway that bridged over the canal. I labeled that location also as "THREE—Angela's head discovered (1992)." I also added the location where an elderly homeowner a few miles west of Angela's murder had found a large plywood board in his alley next to garbage cans with "I chopped that bitches head off" written in red lipstick. I labeled it "FOUR—plywood clue (1992)."

Now that I had the main persons involved listed and the map drawn on the whiteboards, I stepped back and massaged my right hand. I saw the multiple piles of developed 35mm pictures from the murders. Some of the pictures from Angela's murder were labeled "Aerial" (they had been taken from the helicopter), with another large group labeled as being taken from the ground. There were also autopsy photos and photos from the scene where her head was recovered. The pictures from Melanie's murder were similarly labeled but included pictures from inside a tunnel nearby. I then carefully placed them in what I believed to be sequential or logical order, thumbtacking them to the bulletin board on the other side of my newly created war room.

Tired from this tedious endeavor, I sat down in a metal chair and stared at the massive collection of photos. *Man, it's painful to see what the monster did to these innocent girls.* I looked at my watch and couldn't read the numbers. I rubbed my eyes and tried again. The worn silver watch face blurred but still read 1 A.M. *No wonder.* Case or no case, sleep was imperative now so I could focus. I gathered my backpack and coat and headed toward the door. Before the lights were turned out, I looked back at the fruits of my labor and grinned. *The picture was beginning to coalesce. It always did. I would get this son of a bitch.*

The next morning (really, later that same morning), it was lather-rinse-repeat. Eggs, bacon, and coffee and the big room. I digested the find-the-hidden-object collage from the day before and took some comfort in it, but there was a lot more to do in building the visualization of the incident. I wanted to examine the similarities of the murders. I found an open section of whiteboard and wrote "Similarities." Both women had their clothing torn and cut at some point during the murder. Both victims were on a bike path near a canal riding their bikes at dusk. Also, there were tunnels nearby both murder scenes. Both women had a fatal stab wound to their upper back, which immediately collapsed their lungs and penetrated their hearts. Both women's mountain bikes as well as Sony Walkman cassette players were taken from the scene and never found. The strangest of similarities had to do with both women wearing their shoes and socks.

More coffee, more shaking out of a cramped right hand. I continued to write. However, I transitioned to "Dissimilarities." Our first victim, Angela, was beheaded. Melanie was not. Angela was deeply cut in the shape of a cross across her abdomen postmortem. It appeared the killer may have been trying to cut Angela in half. *Disturbing at all levels!* The killer also used what appeared to be another instrument besides a knife and drove holes in her pelvic area.

This heavy mutilation was not the case with our second victim, Melanie. With her, the killer made a slight incision across her neck and carved a cross with three dots within. He also carved the letters *WSC* into Melanie's center chest. Angela was displayed on a berm naked facing east (with only her shoes and socks), whereas Melanie was re-dressed by the killer into a small girl's aqua bodysuit. She was dragged a considerable distance and placed in the canal. There was considerable graffiti inside a tunnel near Melanie's murder, whereas this was not found at Angela's. I shook my head in disgust for what had been done and because I was still lost and no closer to the killer than when I began.

With the most painful part done, I used the restroom, and then realized that I was starving. I sat at one of the center tables and ate a peanut-butter-and-grape-jelly sandwich my wife made me that morning. Something as simple as a PB&J always seemed to taste better when she made it. It was good to remember my loved ones during these dark, arduous hours. I cleaned the last remnants of peanut butter and jelly from my hands and got back to writing.

I wrote "What's Been Done—Angela." Detectives canvassed her apartment complex and the surrounding area. Most people were asleep or not home. Neighbors did see Angela leave the apartment with a described "angry" look. Also, a couple going to a convenience store at 1 A.M. the night of the murder saw a thin man looking around and holding something in his jacket and using both hands to cradle it. Another couple saw a man acting strangely and attempting to enter the front door of a church near the scene. This man had something in his right hand.

Additionally, detectives spoke to Angela's coworkers at Syntellect. They gave a consistent story of Angela wanting to leave Joe. A large number of tips came in from around the country and from field contacts with officers reporting a strange person, bike, or vehicle sighting, known creepy subjects, killers from around the country, and so on. The detectives organized and completed tracking packets and then triaged and vetted.

A few weeks after Angela's murder, detectives flew to Los Angeles, visited the *Los Angeles Times* headquarters, and systematically interviewed the employees who attended Angela's training seminar. Detectives also went to the apartment complex where Angela resided while finishing up her studies at DeVry. They interviewed Angela's adviser and her professor and obtained a list of students who attended DeVry at the same time. They also interviewed and obtained a blood sample from a former boyfriend of Angela's at DeVry who denied involvement and had no motive.

I took a break to get some air. When I came back, I looked at the scribbles on the dry-erase boards all over the room. *It looked like a mathematician who'd gone insane trying to prove a hellacious theory.* New marker; *keep going.*

I started in on the next section with "What's Been Done—Melanie's Murder."

Detectives canvassed the scene, and inexplicably no one saw or heard anything. *No one? Seriously? He took a ton of time with both of these girls, and no one saw or heard anything?* Numerous tips came in and were doggedly followed up on. An FBI profile on both murders was completed in the mid-1990s. DNA from semen at both scenes was matched to the same unknown killer and in the late-1990s it was uploaded into the national DNA database. There had been no hits to the DNA in the federal database to date.

After many hours of tedious work spanning days, I stared at the whiteboards and photos. I had summarized every pertinent detail from the massive reports. I looked back and forth repeatedly for the hidden clue that would break the case wide open. *Where in the hell was it? Nothing. Was the visual every-debit-has-a-corresponding-credit exercise all done for nothing? Should I assume the monster is dead, like all the others do?*

No, no, no! I couldn't give up on these women and their families. I just needed help. I needed to assemble a team of elite investigators.

CHAPTER 4
THE TEAM

The DNA Expert

T he crowd of detectives peppered Kelley Merwin with questions, and her zeal for the subject, paired with almost twenty years of lab experience, blanketed the room. Most of us did not have a scientific background. High school chemistry was the best we had to offer. Somehow, in less than an hour, she broke down the rather complex world of DNA in a manner a child could easily understand. She compared it to a blueprint for a house or code for a video game. *Excellent!* We appreciated it. We depended on DNA to solve our cases. DNA had become a game-changer in the fight against crime. It had evolved dramatically since the time of the canal murders and continued to get more precise.

I was pleased I had carved out time to attend Kelley's brown-bag-lunch lecture that day, and I approached her after the crowd dispersed. We became friends during my assignment in cold case homicide. Her husband was an affable top-notch officer I had worked with in the past. Not to mention, Kelley and I shared supervisory philosophies. We both believed in finding the best people and getting out of their way. She knew we carried a heavy load of 2,500-plus cold cases on our records and made it abundantly clear she and her team were there to help us.

"Let me see a picture of Morty," I said.

"Here's Morty," said Kelley. She set her phone down in front of me.

"He's a good-looking dog! Markings like Steve." Steve was my English bulldog. Unfortunately, he had passed away a few years back.

"Does Morty snore?" I asked.

"Oh, yeah, he wakes us up in the middle of the night sometimes."

"And passes gas at about the same rate?"

She laughed. "Yes, Morty is quite proficient at that, too."

"They're the perfect breed. Lazy as can be, and they don't want much out of life but to eat, sleep, and be loved."

Kelley showed me several more pictures of Morty. Morty was a bright spot in her crime-fighting world. The Halloween and play pictures made me laugh.

"Now that I think of it," I said, "good ol' Steve liked his tug-of-war with his rope, too. The darn dog would not, under any circumstance, let go of it."

"Stubborn breed. They don't give up."

"They're bred to pull bulls, get thrown off, and go right back at it. That's the way I want my cold case team to be," I said.

"And how is that coming along?" Kelley asked.

"I'll get to that in a minute. Do you remember the canal murders?"

"Yes, I worked on the DNA for those cases years ago. Angela Brosso and Melanie Bernas. November 1992 and September 1993. Serial killer stuff like decapitation, carving, re-dressing."

Kelley then launched into a series of details on both cases that only the original investigators would know. It was evident her memory was a steel trap.

"Do you remember the details on all of your cases like this?" I asked.

"Well, yes, it's kind of a gift. But these are two of the most, if not the most, horrific murders in our city and the State of Arizona, for that matter."

"Yes, they are, indeed. I just spent weeks locked in a room walking through them step by step. I thought I could use my CPA-nerd organizational skills to find the missing clue."

"Did you?" Kelley asked.

"Um, no, that's why I'm over here talking to this intelligent DNA supervisor who doesn't miss a detail. Would you join my team to solve them? I need to assemble a team of the best to even have a chance against a serial killer."

Kelley beamed. "Yes, of course. I am definitely on board. You do know that the only way you're ever gonna solve the canal murders is to bring us his DNA? The unidentified sample has been in the national CODIS database since 1999 and never matched."

"Okay, that's great news!"

"Do you think he's dead?"

"That seems to be the consensus with the older homicide detectives. I'm not so sure. He could have moved around the country or even world without being detected."

"Definitely," she said.

Kelley's cell phone rang, and she told the caller she would meet her in a nearby lab room. She motioned for me to follow her. From the second-floor balcony, I saw the intricate art display that adorned the main entrance. Items associated with a forensic lab, such as beakers, flasks, pipettes, and wash bottles were suspended in a massive visual collage. I loved to stare at it every time I entered. It creatively defined the lab.

We entered a room that held signs warning not to enter the adjacent room unless properly equipped. I heard Kelley speak to one of her staff. It sounded like she was explaining a process in detail. The staff member couldn't stop telling Kelley how much she appreciated her help. A novice could see that Kelley's knowledge was as important as one of the steel pillars holding the new forensic center in place. They were lucky to have her institutional knowledge and leadership.

We left the room. Kelley apologized for the interruption and said, "Back to the canal murders. What were you saying?"

"I don't see how a person starts off so vicious, cutting off a head and doing what he did to Angela, kills Melanie in an equally awful manner, and then just stops. No similar murders before or after. Or at least that we can find. Just two in a matter of months and then flatline."

"It's so weird. Who else have you picked for your special team?"

"Well, you, and to be determined on the rest. I'll let you know."

The PhD Detective

William Schira let out a groan as he stretched in the doorframe of the office. Years of wearing a gun belt and a couple of accidents as a motorcycle cop had wreaked havoc on his lower back. Stubborn as a mule, though, he didn't skip a beat and hardly ever took a day off from chasing bad guys throughout his long career.

"You ready, boss man?" he asked.

"Yeah, let's go," I said.

We made our way out of headquarters. William stopped and talked to person after person. He reminded me of my mother, who would leave me in the car in the grocery parking lot as a teenager. She would always say, "Troy, I'll be right back." Two to three hours later she would arrive to a steaming mad son. This was before the days of smartphones. It was me, the radio, and my thoughts. I believed she talked to absolutely everyone in the darn store. William would have done the same.

"Do you know everyone in the building, William?"

"Well, boss man, I've been around the block. Lots of time and people since the eighties. Drug enforcement, motors [traffic], NET [neighborhood enforcement team] . . ."

We finally exited the headquarters building, and ten to fifteen other people talked to him. We eventually crossed the road and headed for the crime laboratory.

"You have a pleasant way about you, William. That's for sure."

"If you say so. My father was a dentist, so he had to be nice to people, and maybe it rubbed off on me."

"Is that why your homicide solve rate is so high?"

"Seems like the bad guys just like to tell me things."

We made our way into the conference room, and William exchanged pleasantries with the lab team. Not surprisingly, he seemed to know each like they were old high school friends. It made me laugh.

He was there to present a case to the lab for DNA and fingerprints. Kelley led the meeting as the DNA supervisor. These meetings were a new technique that fostered brainstorming and collaboration between the investigator and the lab personnel. William went over his case in significant detail. At that moment, I learned almost every case William worked would have nicknames. In this one, he described how some guy named Puppet murdered some guy named Clown with the help of Smiley and Joker.

"So, Puppet is your suspect? How do you know?" Kelley asked with a degree of sarcasm.

William slid his bifocals down to the bridge of his nose and said, "Well, I only have a PhD, plain high school diploma, that is, and Puppet himself told me he did it. I just need some more lab work to prove it to the attorney's liking."

We all laughed. William was one of a kind. He would play dumb and joke about having no advanced schooling, but the man was smart as a whip and knew how to get people to talk. Puppet fell prey to William's cunning nature, and there were many, many more who would do so.

When we wrapped up the meeting, Kelley said, "Any new additions to your canal murders team?"

I said, "As a matter of fact, PhD boy over here would be a perfect addition."

William said, "I thought you'd never ask. I was a part of the group who searched the canals after it happened. I spent a ton of time on those cases."

I looked at Kelley and said, "You see, there you have it. You, me, and Puppet's best friend, William. More to follow."

The Passionate One

I walked past Marianne Ramirez's cubicle, and it was, as usual, a beehive of activity. I heard her speaking rapidly on the phone in Spanish. Marianne was a critical member of the International Criminal Apprehension Team, which concentrated primarily on suspects who fled to Mexico. She somehow balanced this taxing assignment with cold cases and supported the rest of the homicide unit with a host of duties. When I walked back through the aisle, she was comforting a victim's mother on the phone in English. It was well known that the mothers all loved Marianne. In fact, when I first opened her personnel file, I noticed volumes of letters from mothers thanking Marianne for her passion and kindness. I could feel the positive energy radiate from her. *A busy, busy Marianne as usual*, I thought and headed for my office. I figured I could talk to her about a high-profile case for an update tomorrow.

I was calmly gathering my phone and backpack to leave when Marianne abruptly entered the office and spewed a bunch of words. She somehow covered about ten key topics in the time it took my blood pressure to descend to normal.

I would always say, "Marianne, what are you talking about? Preface, please. Give me a topic and then tell me." It didn't bother me at all. It was just her way.

She would always grin and reply, "I know, boss, but there's so much to do. I just need to tell you a whole lot in a little amount of time. Then, I need to go handle another hundred things."

"I hear you, but I've got twenty-five hundred cold cases that we're all trying to work on. I get confused easily."

"Okay, I'll work on it."

"You do cover a ton of ground daily. So, you need to travel with the attorney general's office on the Arcieri case?" I asked. Marianne was handpicked by the upper chain of command to work on this high-profile case. Robert Arcieri had faked his own death in the late 1980s and tried to avoid pending charges on an intricate murder-for-hire plot relating to a business associate. Marianne had worked tirelessly over the previously few months with the attorney general's office investigators to track him down and hold him accountable after all this time. The elite team was close to an arrest and extradition. In fact, Marianne made such a great impression that they wanted her to come work for them.

"Yeah, boss. I just told you about it."

"You mean when you burst through the door a few minutes ago? I got about two words out of that whole speech. Anyway, the past few days my phone has rung off the hook from our pilots up in the air unit. They wanted to make it clear they can fly you wherever you need to go for that case and apparently any other case." I thought this was rather comical. It would almost take an act of the good Lord for a male detective to get a call back from these guys. Yet, they pined over her beauty like high school boys. Other envious detectives would joke that it should be called Marianne Airlines.

"Oh, and boss, I've been asked by another sergeant to help one of their detectives on a forensic interview of a child. With my experience and all."

"Sure. You do phenomenal interviews."

"I had some good practice when I worked in child crimes and Maryvale Precinct."

"Those had to be extremely tough but rewarding assignments," I said.

"Yes, I learned a lot and thank the Lord to be blessed to work with great people." Marianne always exuded a very positive approach to life.

"Marianne, while we are on the topic of tough but rewarding assignments, I would like you to join me on the canal murders team. I spent weeks in a locked room trying to figure it out myself and realized that I need help. It's Kelley from the lab and William, so far. Thoughts?"

"Yes, of course, boss! I would love to work together on a big investigation with a team."

"Excellent! I would like you and William to scour the original reports and figure out what DNA has not been collected. Figure out who is creepiest and travel wherever you need to get their DNA. Kelley has agreed to fast-track the testing."

William walked into my office. "You hear that, William? We will be flight buddies on the canal murders soon!"

"On Marianne Airlines or commercial? I told Sarge whatever it takes to finally solve them," William said.

The Organizer

The path to my office took me by Mark Armistead's cubicle. There were piles upon piles upon piles of both handwritten and typed papers inside and out of unmarked file folders with no apparent semblance of order. In fact, the piles were at least two-to-three-feet high in all directions, including on the floor and under the desk. I was amazed any adult could fit, let alone function, inside the cubicle. Additionally, a collection of sticky notes blanketed both of Mark's computer screens. The cubicle was not dirty, but it was cluttered beyond clutter.

Both Marianne and William suggested that Mark join our canal murders team to get us organized. We were told the canal murders boxes and files sprawled from our floor to the deepest corners of the basement. I scoffed. *How could this guy with the cluttered desk get us organized on such a large scale? Seriously?*

Before I extended the invitation, I tested him. Mark would crack a smile and say, "Sarge, at any given point in time, I know exactly where everything is." Time after time, whenever I needed even so much as a morsel of information, Mark located and brought it forth expeditiously, smiling and gloating, "You see, I'm organized."

"But your desk does not jibe with any form of organization."

"Maybe I keep it that way so everyone, including supervisors, thinks I'm busy and don't bug me."

"So, you appear like an unorganized mess but are truly super organized?"

"You got me!"

"That's how you did it on the warrant project, too, eh? The young team didn't bug you with stupid questions. You singlehandedly tracked the fugitive down with your knowledge of search engines and told them exactly where to find the fugitive. They made the arrest and took the glory."

"I don't need the glory, and I like to appear cluttered."

"How would you like to join the canal murders team?"

"I'll think about it." He smiled. "Joking. Yes, I would love to help. Marianne and William already asked me. I am old like William and helped canvass on those investigations back in the early 1990s. As a father, I find what happened to those young girls horrific."

"The original reports reference a list of names that stemmed from citizens or other law enforcement agencies or people contacted by the police in the canal area. The detectives triaged the list during the aftermath. Can you get me the list?"

"I'll find it."

The Serial Killer Detective

The sun poured into my office every afternoon, so I could always tell when someone was in the doorway. This shadow was bigger than most. Clark Schwartzkopf's six-foot-two-inch frame created almost a total eclipse.

"Boss, you got a minute? I want to show you something."

"Sure."

"Can we go to the basement?"

"Basement? You and Mark seem to be quite fond of the basement."

"It's quiet and more spacious than my little cubicle."

When we walked past Clark's cubicle, I pointed to his trash can. The can was overflowing with empty water bottles.

"I know you're a runner and all, but how much water do you drink in a day?" I asked.

Clark looked at me intensely and said, "I'm going to file a complaint. Those pigs! They come into the conference room with their potlucks. Most people would just throw the bottles into the large can next to the damn door. Oh, not them! Not these filthy people! No, they go out of their way to dump all of them in mine. I mean, look at this shit. Come on!"

I couldn't help but laugh. Clark exuded tremendous passion for doing things the right way, and he expected the same from other people. I shared this passion.

"Should we cancel all future potlucks?"

"Yes, let those clowns trash someone else's workspace. We're solving murders."

"So, the water bottle trash display didn't block my view of the newspaper article. You took down the serial shooters in the mid-2000s?"

Clark's anger shifted to excitement. "Yes, those dirtbags thought they would never get caught. They just went around shooting people and animals for years. They killed or injured thirty-five victims. A tragedy."

I had triggered another passion of Clark's. Even with over twenty years on the job, he loved to catch the bad guy—a mark of a true detective.

"Remind me of their names again?"

"Dale Hausner and Samuel Dieteman. May they rot in hell!"

"That's impressive."

"Thanks, boss. It was a hell of an investigation. I will write a book about it when I retire. The world needs to be reminded periodically of how hard detectives work to make it safe."

"I agree. That's awesome."

The basement smelled of mildew, but it was indeed spacious and quiet. We entered an unmarked room packed with bankers boxes and binders stacked neatly on shelving units. In the middle, I saw a large table and a single chair. Paperwork was neatly stacked and covered the entire table.

"This is what I wanted to show you. You remember how you gave me that nineties case with the businessman murdered close to headquarters on Grand Avenue?"

"The one that tons of detectives worked through the years and is unsolvable?"

"It's solvable, boss."

"What? I even looked at that case myself. The business partner did it, but there's no evidence and no eyewitnesses."

"That's why I needed space. I took everything I could find. I laid it out and found what we were missing."

I looked at the bulletin board in the corner with a collage of old photos. "You put those up, too?"

"Yes, I had to see everything. Digest it, mull it over, and digest it some more. It proves the business partner was definitely the killer. I disproved any other theories and showed no one else could have done it. It's an ironclad circumstantial case. The county attorney's office said they would charge it. I just need to do a few more things on it."

"I don't know what to say, Clark. That's amazing! You know, I did the same thing on the canal murders. I laid it all out. I looked for days for the missing puzzle piece."

"That's Brosso and Bernas in the early nineties, right? And?"

"Yes. I learned a lot, but I failed. I realized I needed help. I needed a team of the best of the best. You available?"

"I've got a busy schedule with baseball overlapping football. I also need to keep close watch on my financial portfolio."

"Come on! Those women and their families need you."

"I'm joking. I'm in."

The Kid

JJ Alberta suddenly threw down his notes and pursued the prisoner in the orange jumpsuit. The prosecutor with JJ looked on in disbelief. Shouts of "Get him!" from an overweight bailiff echoed as the prisoner sprinted down the hallway in the courthouse. JJ gained on him steadily, but the prisoner had a distinct head start. The prisoner ran through the security area in the lobby, knocked over a woman holding a baby, and continued out the door. He was looking for a getaway vehicle when JJ tackled and handcuffed him. Court security officers surrounded the prisoner, thanked JJ for his efforts, and escorted the prisoner away.

"JJ, are you okay?" asked the female prosecutor.

Out of breath, he said, "I'm a little out of shape since my days in patrol. Okay, but my pants are shredded."

"Aren't you in your twenties? I'm sure your department will buy you some new ones."

JJ said, "Thirties, but my squad nicknamed me the Kid due to my boyish good looks."

"Oh, brother. You are the hero today. That inmate is wanted for armed robbery and murder. He is a very bad dude."

"All in a day's work," said JJ.

"Seriously, though. You're over here testifying on two cold case murders you solved and now you do this heroic act to save society! I need to call your supervisor."

A little while later, JJ walked into my office. I stood up, clapped, and chanted "Hercules" repeatedly.

He laughed. "Aw, it's nothing really. But if Hollywood calls, just have some young stud actor play me."

"One badass detective. I will overlook the fact you went to Michigan State. Seriously, though, nice job, Kid. You're an all-star and put your peers on your former squad to shame. You out-recap them all combined. You have more arrests, more case reviews, and more tasks handled."

"Come on, Sarge, I'm just a simple man trying to make a living."

"I need your help on the canal murders. You heard of them?"

"I was merely an adolescent in middle school, but yes, I've read them both. That's all Marianne talks about, and I figured you would need my expertise."

I laughed. "Indeed. You willing to help?"

"I'm in. I don't want to make anybody look bad, though."

The Dominator

Dominick Roestenberg charged into my office and interrupted. "Sergeant Hillman, sir! I heard you talking with the Kid. I want in, too." With a scowl, he said, "You hear me, Hillman? I want in!"

I remembered much younger versions of Dom and me. We walked into the jail together in uniform and both had prisoners to book. I couldn't get my armed robbery suspect to confess. Within less than five minutes, I looked over and saw Dom high-fiving my suspect and telling him, "It's all good, bro. You did the right thing. You got it off your chest like a man, bro."

He turned to me and said, "He just confessed to the whole thing. I'll write a supplement to your report."

"Wow! Thank you. How did you do that?"

"I've just got a special way, Troy. Special top-secret methods."

"You're a good talker."

I snapped back to Dom's interruption. "I didn't ask you yet, Dom. However, yes, I need both your and JJ's help. You two will follow up on the names Clark and I give you from the files."

"That's easy for the Dominator. We got this!"

"Did you just call yourself the Dominator?"

"That's right!"

"The monster we're looking for on these canal murders may not be as easy to smooth-talk. You're used to robbery suspects. You gonna step up your game?"

"Challenge accepted."

❧

The team was finally assembled for the hunt.

Phenomenal and talented group of people, I thought, *but can we outwit a monster who's been hiding for decades?*

CHAPTER 5
THE FBI PROFILES

I t would be a long and painful exercise, but it needed to be done. I needed to ensure the team read and fully digested the FBI profiles of an array of serial killers. The only way I could do that was to go over the profiles in a group setting led by instructors. Otherwise, even with the greatest of intentions, they may not do it. I knew different team members will often see something that the others may not, and I believed in this type of intense and forced collaboration. The FBI had collected volumes of information on serial killers over the years, and we had nothing. We needed to be armed with this information while we hunted.

I stood in front of the conference room and said, "Thanks, guys, for coming, and we'll try to keep this as brief as possible. I included in your packets last meeting two profiles done by the FBI—one for Angela dated February 22, 1993, and the second for Melanie dated December 12, 1995. The first one was written by a supervisory special agent at Quantico. The second one was drafted by another supervisory special agent who consulted with the agent who wrote Angela's. Overall, I do think that these profiles are solid, and we should look at them as a guide as we move forward. I have asked William to present the profile on Angela, and Marianne to present the one on Melanie. William?" I said.

William pulled his bifocals down to the bridge of his nose. He peered down at the standard-font profile paperwork. "You see this first part—it's more of a hoity-toity FBI disclaimer saying this is just their best guess based on what they've seen."

I smiled, as William loved to pretend he was not at the intelligence level or sophistication of a typical FBI agent. He could match them step for step.

"So, the next part covers victimology. It basically says that 'unsub' [William used his fingers to imitate quotes] Angela would have been 22 years old the day that her body was located. Angela was living with a male and had told her friends that she was going to move out. She had expressed concern in telling him about moving, but also told her friends that she did not think he would harm her. Angela worked for a tech company and was doing well."

"The male was named Joe Krakowiecki, right?" blurted Clark.

"Yeah, it doesn't say that in here, but in the report, that's who her fiancé was," replied William. "Moving on with this victimology, Angela didn't drink much and didn't use drugs. She was described as rather friendly yet slightly naïve by friends. Her social life revolved around her boyfriend and work friends. The FBI considered her lifestyle low risk for violent crime. However, when she went for rides on her bike, it put her in what they called 'situationally higher risk level.'"

William continued, "So, the next category looks at the medical examiner's report. They do their special FBI disclaimer saying basically that this is not to redo the medical report but rather to show the 'significance' of the injuries. They refer to the initial wound as 'stab wound number 1,' which was to the back and fractured the tenth rib, punctured the left lung, and penetrated the descending aorta. The author believed that this wound was 'consistent' with Angela being on her bike at the time. He believed it was what he called a 'blitz-style attack' and was the fatal injury. The author referenced a superficial stab wound on the back side of victim near her butt area. He made note of the 'abrasive' injuries to Angela's left leg and thigh area and lower back and butt area as being consistent with being dragged by the perpetrator from her bike to the area where she was found. It was at this location that the killer cut off her clothing, stabbed and cut the victim, and then beheaded her. He was acting out his 'violent fantasy' at this point."

"Violent fantasy is no joke, holy crap," bellowed Dom, looking around at his peers.

William continued, "The FBI guy concludes this section with a statement saying that the killer had a large sharp cutting instrument and has 'considerable' strength."

"I would have to agree. Considerable strength is right on the mark as he dragged her for a long way along the path, up a berm, and then began cutting on her," I said.

William nodded, stretched his back slowly as he gritted his teeth, and said, "Agreed. Now, moving on with my part. This FBI fellow then goes into what he calls the 'crime assessment.' Here, he talks about the killer's violent fantasy, which gives the killer what he calls 'erotic satisfaction and pleasure.' He goes on to say that the crime was disorganized, and the killer attacked a victim of opportunity rather than a target, as Angela had just arrived home from a business trip and went on an evening bike ride. The FBI profiler believes that the killer waited on or near the bike path and did a blitz-style attack from behind. He thinks that Angela tried to escape but was not able to do so because of the fatal stab wound. Any questions so far, guys and gal?"

Everyone shook their heads, looking intently down at their sheets. The brutality was a step further, or maybe incalculable steps further, than other homicide investigations we had dealt with in the past.

"Okay, the FBI guy goes back over him dragging her to the location where she was found and cutting off her clothes. He then talks about the killer making two incisive cuts across the top of her chest and then down the center to the genital area. The profiler guy notes two stab wounds on each side of the large cut down the center above the genital area. He said only the killer would know what that meant. He then describes a 'transverse incisive cut' on Angela's upper left chest area, as if the killer was trying to remove skin or expose organs. The killer cut deeply and completely around her torso at the waistline before cutting off her head. He believed that this suggests 'curiosity, experimentation, and desire to satisfy the personal needs of the offender.' What he called the true significance of all this would only be known by the killer."

"I still can't believe what he did to these girls," said Mark.

"I can't either, Mark. It's tragic," Marianne said.

William adjusted his glasses and said to Marianne, "Next slide please."

"Okay, okay, Mr. Patience," said Marianne.

"The profile goes into the sexual nature of the crime and indicates that sex may not necessarily have taken place, but there may have been mastur-bation and semen present as he lived out the violent fantasy."

Dom whispered a long drawn-out, "Sicko for sure."

William continued, "Moving on. So this author says that a killer usually removes body parts either to delay IDing the victim or for what they call personal reasons. Since the killer didn't cut off the hands and feet, the FBI profiler believed that the killer took the head for 'personal needs' to satisfy his fantasy. Once the satisfaction was gone, he threw the head into the canal. The bike path being highly used makes this a 'very high-risk crime' for the killer. The profiler believed that the killer may have been impulsive in fulfilling his fantasy but was aided by darkness and the berm. He also said that this mutilation would have taken a lot of time. The killer would have had a lot of blood on him, and the head would be difficult to carry and conceal. The profiler believed that the killer walked to the scene and then took the victim's bicycle to leave the scene."

"Any questions so far?" I asked.

Everyone shook their heads and stared down.

"Next, the FBI guy looked at the offender characteristics and traits. He believes this to have been committed by a white male, based on their research. The author disclaims that making an age determination is hard, but the behavior in this murder usually manifests in the late twenties.

They targeted our killer at late twenties to late thirties and described him as 'a loner, stays to himself, unusual, strange, eccentric, not a neat dresser, disheveled, sloppy.' The profile says that our killer lacks interpersonal skills and has few if any close friends; he would associate with people much older or younger than him. He would live alone or with a 'parental figure.'"

"Like Norman Bates," said JJ.

"Oh, Kid, let William go on so he can get his lunch," said Marianne, smiling.

William rubbed his belly and continued. "So, they said he would be familiar with the scene due to living, working, or frequently visiting the area. He would be working in unskilled or semi-skilled labor, if employed. Our killer would engage in walking as a means of getting around and do so at night. He would have an older vehicle but not well maintained. The killer may have taken clothing or jewelry so that he could relive his fantasy. The FBI believes that this violent of a crime would have been triggered by a significant stressor. They cannot rule out mental illness, but the killer functions okay in society to avoid detection. He may have been counseled or institutionalized in the past."

I could tell the group was on overload, but we needed to let this important information marinate.

"The next section covers 'post offense behavior.' The author said that the killer would have taken the head to a location where he felt safe, using the victim's bike, to complete his fantasy. The killer would have needed to be alone for some time to 'decompress,' and this would be in an area where he would have no concern about interruption. The killer would have been bloody and needed to change clothes and clean up. FBI research suggests that he would dispose of body parts to leave a message or to shock and offend. As to why he chose the canal, the FBI guy said only the killer would know, but it appears he wanted to make sure it was found and send a message. Finally, the profiler said the killer would take a high level of interest in the crime and/or progress of the investigation."[1]

"Wow! That was a bunch of information, William. Good work on walking us through it. Any questions from the team?" I asked.

Everyone was silent. I wasn't sure if it was because of the gravity of the material or because they were just beginning to get hungry for lunch.

"My turn," piped in Marianne, energetic and cheerful as always. "The agent who wrote this one said he took into consideration Angela's profile and would look at similarities. Like the one William just went over, they start with victimology. Melanie was seventeen years old and was last seen by her mother at their home when she left at nineteen hundred hours. When her mother returned, Melanie was not there, and her mountain bike was also missing. Melanie was a good student, only drank on occasion, and did not use drugs. She rode her bike for physical activity. She would be considered low risk for violent crime. However, she went for a ride on a bike at night near an area where another woman was killed. The FBI says this put her at the 'situationally higher risk level'—just like Angela. Any questions?"

Everyone shook their heads.

"Okay, so next they covered the medical examiner's report, and like with Angela they put in their disclaimer. They describe the initial stab wound as being 'almost identical' to the one to Angela regarding location, dimensions, and no other wounds to the back. Like Angela, Melanie was dragged from the point where she collapsed to a nearby location, which was concealed from people walking or riding by on the path. All the cutting and activities committed on both girls were done after death. On Melanie, the cutting and sexual activity was done prior to re-dressing. The FBI noted an incision on her neck that went all the way across. The killer cut the letters *WSC* between and slightly above her breasts. They were not very deep, indicating the killer was careful and focused while cutting. The FBI indicated that the act of re-dressing Melanie into a one-piece bathing suit was a violent sexual fantasy. All these activities suggested the killer spent a lot of time at the crime scene."

"A real sick puppy," threw out William.

Marianne nodded in agreement. "On to the next part, which is crime scene analysis. The FBI said that the bike path was well lit and near a busy highway. Melanie did not bike this way often. They believed that she was a victim of opportunity and that the killer selected both girls based on being on the bike path on a mountain bike. The killer took a greater risk in choosing the girls on bikes rather than someone on foot. They said that this approach of killing them on the bike may be part of his fantasy. In both murders, the killer inflicted a single stab wound to the back in a 'blitz-style attack.' He dragged Melanie to a private location along the path, as he did with Angela, and cut off her clothing. At this point, the FBI said that there was 'divergence in behavior.' They suggested that the mutilation was not as extensive as with Angela, but it was part of his fantasy and 'eroticized.' Evidence suggests that the killer obtains sexual gratification from the violent acts."

"Apparently, he's wired differently from the rest of us," said William.

"Apparently." I nodded in agreement. "Marianne, moving on . . ."

"The FBI believes that the act of re-dressing in a turquoise bathing suit that was way too small took a long time and was 'paramount' to him in his fantasy. The killer is described by the FBI as disorganized, but the act of bringing the bathing suit showed some degree of organization. Next, they look at the *WSC*, the cross, and the neck incisions, suggesting that they were done with 'great care.' They believed the killer engaged in this 'ritualistic behavior' as part of his fantasy."

Dom added a few court jester thoughts. We rolled our eyes. This information was very heavy, and most of us needed some humor. Humor that he provided.

"Okay, so the FBI believes that there is an 'association' with water in both cases. With Angela, the killer took her head and then risked discovery when throwing it into the canal. He could have easily disposed of it in a safer manner but chose this method. With Melanie, he dragged her from concealment in the bushes to the canal and threw her into the water. He risked being seen. The FBI thinks that the water was not designed to get rid of evidence but rather part of his fantasy and coined it 'ritual behavior' only known to the killer. This was high-risk behavior given that the bike path was well-lit, there was a lot of blood on the trails, he moved the body several times, and the amount of time spent with both victims. They describe him as 'impulsive' with an 'intense obsession of fulfilling his fantasy.' The killer took both bikes and Walkmans as apparent souvenirs. He could then relive his fantasy."

The team sat still and absorbed the massive amount of information.

"Okay, now on to 'offender characteristics and traits.' They believe that the killer is familiar with the area where Melanie was killed as well as Angela's scene. He frequented there, often feeling comfortable there, and people would have seen him there before. They go on to say that the killer may be a mental health patient under care. With the 'success' of both murders, the fantasies would become more 'elaborate.' There is strong likelihood that he was hospitalized or incarcerated after Melanie's murder, as there haven't been any more of these types of crimes—that was in 1995 when this was written."

"Yeah, it's so bizarre that he does two horrific murders in close proximity and then just stops," I said.

"So, one theory is that he's hospitalized in a mental institution or in prison," Clark said.

William jumped in: "If he's in a mental institution, then getting his DNA is virtually impossible. I have tried to get them to allow for DNA collection, but the powers that be will have none of it."

"That's concerning that our killer could be institutionalized, and we will never get his DNA," I said.

"Tell me about it," said William.

"Kelley told me that if he's in prison, then his DNA should have hit to our unknown crime scene sample in CODIS," said Marianne.

"One would think, but can we be sure?" I asked.

Marianne shook her head dismayed. "She said that the DOC is pretty good about swabbing the prisoners, but they have been known to miss a few." She was referring to the Department of Corrections.

"Ugh," I muttered.

Marianne continued, "Another theory is that he moved on to other parts of the state or country. And the final theory that was held by the original scene agent and many others is that he's dead."

"That's the million-dollar question then: Why did he stop?" Mark said.

"Or did he?" Clark said.

"There's one last part, and then I'm done with this profile," said Marianne. "The FBI believed that he would have a collection of violent pornography, including detective-type magazines. The knife used in both murders would be important to him. They did not believe he would have disposed of it.[2] And, that's it. Round of applause, please!"

"I applaud the fact that I'm going to lunch now," said William.

"Thanks again, guys. That was a ton of information. Let it marinate in those brilliant minds of yours, and we'll discuss next week."

"Brilliant?" said Dom.

"He's talking about me," said JJ.

"Kid! It's not always about you!" said Marianne.

CHAPTER 6
THE CLUES AND THE
MEDICOLEGAL DEATH EXAMINER

D usk was typically my favorite time of the day. It was my time to unwind from the day's chaos. But not that night. I felt a tinge of reluctance with a stronger dose of excitement. The reluctance stemmed from whether I could handle all that. Police work had made me tough. However, what the killer did to those girls was a dark fantasy on such a high level that it cut right through the shields I had put up. But the excitement to explore further and discover something I or someone else missed kept me going. I spent countless hours inside the confines of a large room and reconstructed the murders from scratch. I knew I needed to get closer. I needed to feel and embrace the scenes.

I parked my truck in a deserted lot near the dog park and grabbed my flashlight, a file folder, and a pad of paper. According to my map and the pictures, I was due east of where Melanie's attack took place, the tunnel that held the graffiti, and the freeway. Not much had changed since that horrific September day in 1993. Some plants had been cut back or moved, but for the most part, things appeared the same. I plodded along the canal trail bank toward the setting sun and watched the murky water flow steadily on my left. I couldn't control the urge to periodically look over my shoulder. I felt very alone here. The spilled blood had long ago been scrubbed away, yet I still knew it was there, and so did the killer. *Maybe he had been here recently? How often had he come back to the scene to relive his wretched fantasy?*

"On your left," a male voice hollered. I quickly moved right but dropped my pad of paper. The biker breezed by me and into the setting sun. I stood startled for a few moments and looked back toward where the biker came from and the lights of central Phoenix. I imagined Melanie pedaling toward me. *Why had she stopped? Had she also yelled "on your left," but our killer didn't heed it?* Melanie had scuff marks on the back of her legs, so she may have crashed her bike attempting to avoiding hitting the monster. These could have been caused by the killer dragging her, though. Her bike was never found, so there were no answers there, either. *Or did he use a plea-for-help ruse to get her to stop and get off her bike?* Ted Bundy used it in his murders. Our killer could have done the same. I had so many questions.

I looked at the photos in an envelope labeled "Melanie—Scene" to ensure I was in the right spot. This had to be close to the area on the trail where he got her off her bike and stabbed her. I looked west toward the tunnel. The killer dragged Melanie's lifeless body a considerable distance to the area right outside of the tunnel and bushes. I edged toward this area in what was now blackness and shined my light. The bushes were no longer there. I felt a pit in my stomach. This is where he raped and re-dressed her.

I would explore the tunnel in a bit. I needed to follow his next move. I looked back at the scene photos to refresh my memory. I walked south toward the canal bank and then a considerable distance west to the edge of the canal. He pulled her from the bushes, dragged her along the canal bank, and pushed her in the canal at about this spot, I figured. *How did he carry her all this way? And for what purpose? Why did no one see this? It was dark out there, but I did not understand how there were no witnesses.* I heard the incessant rumble of cars passing along I-17 to my left. The moonlight danced on the canal water, but the air was tight.

I walked back from the canal toward the bike path and tunnel and took a sharp left. The tunnel was designed for pedestrians and bikes to pass underneath the freeway. I trudged into the belly of the pedestrian tunnel. The air was stale, and the fluorescent lights hummed. I pulled out another envelope of pictures, which read "Melanie—Tunnel Pics." There were thirty or so photos in the folder, and I noted that the interior tunnel area in 1993 appeared like tonight, relatively well lit with powerful halogen fixtures on the ceiling at regular ten-foot intervals. Apparently, not much had changed here, either, in the last twenty years.

On the north side in the photos, the markings painted on the smooth gray walls were in black paint and denoted with various fonts and shapes: "Mini Park, La Raza, Gumby, by VMPL's, XXV3." Yet, on the south side, the markings were different, resonant in crimson red. This looked like something. From left to right, the crimson markings read *"WSC, KAW, Blitz, Little Devil, TWEETY"* (the *T* was distinctive, almost like the Greek letter tau, the *W* matched the *WSC* on the walls and on Melanie's body, and the *Y* had a unique circle at the bottom) with the *Tweety* immediately followed by a cartoon-type character of a man wearing a fedora and eyeglasses. It almost looked like a detective, of a sort.

After looking at the photos, I continued scribbling feverishly.

- Why did the killer write *WSC* in dark red (blood/marker/paint?) on tunnel wall? (Melanie's murder)—three places of *WSC*—body, sign, and tunnel wall—major clue?
- Why did he write *Tweety*? What does it mean?
- What is the relevance of the man in the fedora?
- Any meaning to other markings of *KAW*, *Blitz*, or *Little Devil*?

I leaned against the tunnel wall, and my mind raced. It was all toxically overwhelming. The wall felt cold to my touch. I wished the walls would warm up and tell me why the killer was so fond of the tunnel and why he lingered there. *Somehow undetected the whole time. Undetected.*

It was getting late, and I knew my wife would be concerned. She knew I had become obsessed with these cases, and she supported me, but I was technically off-duty at night in a rough area of Phoenix. My superiors might think this to be a wacky endeavor. I continued west through the tunnel toward the other side of the freeway and stood at the edge of the canal, gripping my flashlight. This was the scene where the killer had thrown Angela's head into the canal in 1992, almost a year earlier than Melanie's murder. I tried to picture him there, but the setting was bone chilling. Hollywood could not have made it creepier. *Did he pull the head from a bag of some sort? Did he throw it or set it in? He felt extremely comfortable here.*

I wrote:

> Why did the killer take Angela's head and later place it back in the water? Both scenes involved water—why did he deliberately drag Melanie into the water, risking getting caught? Why did he re-dress her in a young girl's swimsuit? what's the fascination? WATER—why, why, why?

The physical act of walking had not taxed me, but the mental load overloaded my circuit board. I had one more stop to make on my nighttime enlightenment tour, though it was not enlightening, by any stretch. I just had more questions. Answers were at a premium in this investigation. I drove a mile north on the freeway to Cactus Road and exited toward Angela's apartment complex. The name had changed, but it was structurally the same, and I pulled into a park near the apartments. The park was still open, but I saw only a few cars scattered in the lot. Before I got out, I remembered reading about how a couple saw Angela race on her bike through this area toward the canal. I would follow her to the monster from here.

I walked through the pedestrian and bike tunnel underneath Cactus Road and continued south on the bike path. No living creatures were around—or at least none that I could see. I stopped and looked at the apartment complex to the west. With my flashlight tucked under my arm,

I pulled out an envelope of pictures labeled "Angela—Scene" and found the area on the berm where her body had been located. I also found a picture of where Angela had been attacked on the bike path. *Right about here.* I trembled. There was no visible presence of the pools of blood on the trail, but I saw them clearly. I followed the blood trail in my mind up the berm. Like he had done with Melanie, he had inexplicably dragged Angela's lifeless body a considerable distance. I stood where I believed he committed the most savage of acts and where he severed her head, and I could not take any more blood and destruction. I needed to leave this place.

I was unsettled by these murders before, but now I plunged deeper. I had been seeking answers but found only more questions. My head ached. I carried on, got back to my truck, and wrote in my notepad.

- Why did the killer use/choose areas near tunnels? Graffiti in tunnel with Melanie and re-dress near tunnel; pedestrian tunnel nearby with Angela. Why?
- Why did he cut their clothing with a knife?
- Why did he leave their shoes and socks on?
- Why did the killer position Angela with her feet to the east? (Possible religious meaning?)
- Why did the killer carve *WSC* between Melanie's breasts? What does it mean?
- Why did he carve a cross with three dots below the *WSC* on Melanie? Why three dots on a cross—meaning?
- Religious significance of cutting on Angela? Two round holes in lower midsection; transection of body—cut like cross? Religion again?
- Why did killer paint/mark a sign near Melanie's scene *93 WSC?*

Tweety, WSC, cross with dots, all those clues, I thought. *What was this monster trying to tell us?*

❧

The next morning, William handed me a large stack of sorted papers.

"What's this?" I asked.

"That's a list of all the Tweety and Little Devil nicknames listed in PACE [our records system at the time]. I looked through them, and nothing really sticks out. Apparently, there's a bunch of gang members named Tweety and Little Devil."

I scrolled through the stack and smiled back. "You know, William, of all of the people on the team, I was absolutely sure you would be the one to lock in on a possible nickname for our bad guy based on the clues."

William stretched with vigor and barked back, "What can I say? All my cases seem to have Puppets, Shortys, and Smileys. And now, possibly Tweety?"

"Well, William, you never know. Thanks for checking out that angle."

I didn't think either of us truly believed that we were going to find that our killer was nicknamed Tweety. It was worth checking, though, and that's the reason William went through the motions on it. Rather, I felt the killer painted Tweety on the concrete walls to mean something else—something of greater significance to him. *But what?*

We learned that the original group of investigators thought the killer may have been trying to throw them off by carving the *WSC* on Melanie's chest. *WSC* was the abbreviation for a large popular gang in Phoenix called West Side City. Neither murder scene was in West Phoenix, but they were reasonably close. I took issue with this possible theory. *If one were to operate on this premise, then why the cross underneath? Were these the initials for another victim?* We scoured our files and the internet for a victim with these initials (and *KAW*, which was painted on the wall also) and came up empty-handed. *Also, why did he use a separate tool like an awl or rounded-tip device to deliberately create three dots within the cross?*

From *Tweety* to *WSC*, the incessant churning of clues continued when I turned to the religious significance of the cross and three dots carved into

Melanie. I searched the internet for the meaning behind the three dots on the cross and ran across some literature suggesting it might be a symbol for the Holy Trinity. Other than that, I found nothing regarding their significance. I was stumped. *It meant something, but what?*

Combining the *WSC* with the cross propelled my research to something called the Westminster Shorter Catechism, which was a simple catechism written in the seventeenth century for the purpose of educating Christian children, especially Presbyterians. With that kernel of information, I read extensively about the catechism over the coming months. The other solution to *WSC* was possibly the Westminster Seminary California. I grew up Presbyterian at the behest of my devout mother, but this was way beyond my scope of knowledge.

I located an advertisement for a church in South Phoenix. The biography on the pastor said he was an expert with the Westminster Shorter Catechism, so I called him. When I tried to explain, he was offended that I would associate the catechism with murder and abruptly ended our conversation. My team later joked that I had upset a pastor. "In pursuit of justice and a higher purpose," I snapped back at them. My next step was to seek out a religious scholar, and I found a professor at a local university in the department of theology. I asked him about *WSC* combined with a cross and three dots, but he could think of nothing relevant. *Frustrating. It has to mean something to the killer. If only we could decode it.*

❧

I reached for the door handle and took a deep breath. It all seemed rather barbaric, like something straight out of a medieval torture chamber, but it was for the greater good. After all, the investigation did not end at the scene. The body itself was riddled with clues that needed to be discovered and could potentially alter the course of an investigation. The tools of the craft alone were enough to haunt even the bravest. The skull key. The brain knife. The rib shears. The tongue tie. The dissection scissors.

The images reappeared every time I grabbed that wretched door handle. It was like my own personal horror film that tirelessly looped. The lifeless body identified only by a toe tag with nothing but time to be probed, dissected, and filleted on the cold metal table. The harvested organs to be delicately weighed. The smell of formaldehyde to torment the nostrils. The ribs that would crack, and the saws that would buzz. I had seen my share of bodies during my police career, but somehow there was a difference between looking at a lifeless body and seeing a human deconstructed piece by piece.

Thankfully, we were not there to observe the dissection of a fellow human. We were at the medical examiner's building to pick the brain—no pun intended—of an expert. Marianne set up a meeting with a new doctor from South America. His official title was medicolegal death investigator, and he was an expert on religion and symbolism. We hoped he could guide us on our troubling clues like what *WSC* meant and why the cross carved into Melanie had three distinct dots. The good doctor could possibly unravel the sick riddles for us.

Even though Marianne and William talked about the fuzzy topics of family and vacations, I was stuck in my horror film with the rows and columns of bodies in sterile metal compartments housed here. I wondered who would want to work in this environment daily. About the only perk I could figure was the constant super-cold temperature that buffered the overbearing Phoenix heat. The doctor entered the front waiting area. He was rather tall and slender and spoke with a distinctive English accent. Prior to our meeting, Marianne had sent him a summary of both cases, the FBI profile, and photos of the victims, along with the original ME's reports.

"Hello, Detectives! Nice to meet you!" he said. He shook our hands firmly and warmly.

"Nice to meet you, Doctor," we said, in turn.

"I've reserved the conference room over here for us." While the doctor escorted us through a variety of hallways to a midsized room, I tried to wall off the chilling images and toxic smells. It didn't work. I decided to concentrate on the cozy confines of the conference room. We sat at a large table surrounded by thick medical books housed on shelf upon shelf. I wondered if doctors read the weighty books or if they just used the internet these days. The room was sparsely decorated, with no living plants. *Fitting*.

The doctor didn't waste any time. "I agree with the profile, but I must say it's not my area of expertise. I do think the suspect had a working knowledge of or education in human anatomy. The stab wounds are too precise for that to not be the case. In looking at all the incisions, it points to someone who knows what they were doing."

"So, maybe a doctor or medical professional?" Marianne asked.

"Quite possibly, but that's not absolute," he said cautiously. "In looking at the *WSC* art and carving, the one that popped out to me was Westminster Shorter Catechism. With the cross involved, I believe this might just be the case. Do you guys know what that is?"

Marianne asked, "Boss, didn't you think that, too?"

"Yeah, I came across it in my research and read up on it," I said. "I'm no expert like yourself, Doctor, but the letters, the cross, and the fact that Melanie was submerged in water and Angela was beheaded, leads me to think this was all some type of religious message."

"That's good," the doctor said. "And to further my point, you remember the spray-painted sign of *93 WSC*?'"

We all nodded affirmatively.

"The ninety-third question in the catechism refers to the sacraments of the New Testament. Those are baptism and the Lord's Supper."

I looked at William and Marianne with an astonished look.

"I'm no scholar, but I thought it was because he killed her in 1993," said William.

"Could be, Detective," the doctor replied, "but I don't think so. I think it's religious. In taking a different approach, these could be runic symbols. The *W* might mean 'Othala' or 'Odal,' which translates to inheritance. This was used by the Nazis when they occupied Croatia. Multiple neo-Nazi groups have championed that symbol. So, basically, your killer could have a knowledge of runic magic or neo-Nazi teachings."

"Runic magic?" I asked as I feverishly wrote down the highlights on my steno pad.

"Well," the doctor said, "the simple answer is Norse mythology. Unfortunately, I am pressed for time this afternoon, or I would absolutely love to tell you all about it."

"I'll just google it, Doctor," I said.

"So," the doctor continued, "the last thing is the cross on your second victim. I think it might represent the symbol for sulfur. Sulfur is a symbol of transformation. Maybe your killer was meaning transformation and rebirth. I mean, making something beautiful out of something that's ugly. If that's not it, then maybe he was referring to one of four different types of crosses: the patriarchal cross from Orthodox Christianity; the cross of Lorraine, which symbolized Joan of Arc and the French; the Salem cross; or the Caravaca cross from the Spanish. I'm not seeing a connection to the Spanish or French one, but I'm gonna say it's still possibly the sulfur symbol."

I wrote in shorthand, and when I looked up at Marianne and William with a you-getting-all-of-this look, they, too, seemed overwhelmed by the litany of information.

The intellectual outpouring continued. The doctor said, "One more thing. If we go down the road of transformation, then you might want to think about the movie *Silence of the Lambs*, as I believe the book was published in 1988 and the movie followed in 1991. The serial killer in that book and movie killed women in search of transformation."

"Wow, um, that's a lot of information, Doctor. I'm very impressed at your knowledge, sir," said Marianne.

"Thank you very much, Doctor," said William.

He replied, "You're very welcome. Please let me know if you think of anything else, and we can meet again when things slow down."

On the way back to headquarters, William blurted out, "Just to get this straight in my pea brain, we're looking for a killer fascinated by baptism, water, and religion, who is a darn good artist, has a runic magic fascination, and leans toward the right as a neo-Nazi."

"And he likes sulfur, transformations, and *The Silence of the Lambs*," Marianne said.

"Pretty much. Let's go find him! Should be simple enough, right?" I said.

I got back to the office and read all about runic magic. Fascinating stuff, but I just didn't see how I could translate it into identifying our killer. I looked out the window overlooking Adams Street and pondered. *The Silence of the Lambs*—that movie troubled me in high school. Sulfur? Transformation? Wow, this was some thick subject matter. *I could use a scotch on the rocks right now*, I thought, and smiled.

I drove away from the office and continued the mental churn of the clues: *What about the other clues he left us? Why re-dress Melanie in a young girl's bodysuit? Why did he leave both shoes and socks on both victims? What did the man in the fedora mean? Or was it really a man in a fedora at all?*

CHAPTER 7

THE MILITARY BADASS, THE BASEMENT, AND THE FILES

I stared out my office window, rocked in my worn government-issued chair, and rhythmically squeezed my blue stress ball. I was feeling both excited and troubled.

"What's troubling my favorite CPA?" a voice said.

I was startled and turned abruptly away from the window. My supervisor, Lieutenant Joe Knott, stood in my doorway. He was of average height and build, but he had a powerful presence. His conservatively parted light brown hair and his carefully groomed mustache complemented his lean and tanned face. The lieutenant was a very well-respected and seasoned veteran on the department who always wore an immaculate button-up shirt and tie, except on the rare occasions he was in a golf polo supporting his favorite cause as a dedicated organizer of a large law-enforcement charity golf event. The lieutenant had worked in all divisions of the department and had the dogged and unyielding edge of a traffic motorcycle cop yet the intelligence and detail-oriented tenacity of an investigator. Not to mention, the admirable lieutenant had an advanced degree in information technology; was extremely savvy in business and finances, to the point where he became visibly excited by Excel spreadsheets; and communicated exceptionally well both verbally and in writing. To boot, the lieutenant would approach the chief's office on the dreaded fourth floor and, with absolute fearlessness, ask for additional resources. He always had an ironclad justification for doing so.

"Hi, LT," I said. "Well, the good news is I have a hungry and talented group of investigators to tackle the canal murders." He knew the basic team, as a solid leader would, but I reiterated their strengths. Mark would be the organizer. Clark would be the one with prior serial killer hunting experience. William would be the plain PhD detective who could interrogate the evilest of tyrants with an unassuming and friendly tenacity. Marianne would balance out the squad with her unwavering passion and enthusiasm. The Kid would provide the ability to juggle hundreds of tasks with utmost efficiency and effectiveness. Dom would be the court jester who could siphon information from any and all leads. And finally, Kelley would be our DNA expert, with her steel trap mind and top-notch collaborative abilities.

He nodded and smiled, "So, I'm not seeing the bad?"

"The bad . . ." I squeezed my stress ball and sighed. "Well, we have some massive challenges in front of us." I told him about how the hundreds of photographs from the crime scenes and autopsies were jumbled and difficult to decipher. There were numerous boxes and binders of documents in multiple locations from the basement to the homicide file room to bookcases outside of detective cubicles. Information was scattered across multiple reports, making it easy to miss something. The state crime lab conducted the original testing, and the transition of the information to Kelley and our crime lab was proving difficult. Many older system reports had been microfiched during that time period. This made searching difficult, to say the least. Newspaper articles were archived and difficult to search. Finally, we had significant time constraints, with 2,500 other cases on our plates. We couldn't just put those cases on hold; that would not be fair to those victims and their families. I was exhausted from just relaying all of this to him.

LT stood there and absorbed every word. He was an excellent listener—a quality missing in many modern-day managers.

"Oh, and everyone over in Homicide and the department, for that matter, seem to think he's dead and that we're wasting our time," I said.

"Are you?" he said.

"I don't believe so. We can't just give up. That's too easy. We have to figure out who did this to these women, even if he is dead. We need to give those families answers, whether he's dead or alive. This, as you know, is Arizona's most terrifying cold case."

"I completely agree. If anyone, and I mean anyone, can figure this out, Troy, it's you and your elite team. I have complete faith in you. It's the fall of 2011. You'll have this knocked out in less than a year," LT said with a comforting smile. I squeezed my little blue ball again and hoped he was right.

᷾

I walked into the conference room and sat down at one of the center tables. I nodded at the group and launched in. "Okay, you are Angela and Melanie's last hope." I scanned the room and ensured strong eye contact. "Now, let's discuss the canal killer and his possible military background. This may help us screen the files for better leads. What say you?"

This meeting was for the team to brainstorm on the distinct possibility our killer was in the military or had prior military training. No one on our team nor any past investigator disputed or dared publicly exclaim that the killer pulled off both murders in a precise and flawless manner, excluding the DNA left at both scenes, of course.

"Well, boss, I definitely think this guy is from the military or has some form of advanced tactical training," said Marianne. Marianne had served in the Navy and developed solid connections over the years with the Naval Criminal Investigative Service (NCIS) in California. She was well versed in the various techniques and training of the various branches. Also, she was studying to be a forensic nurse and had an eye for the detail in forensic trauma.

"So do I," said William. With his years assigned to Homicide, he had a superb eye for scene work.

"And why do you think that?" I asked. I believed it, too, but I wanted to throw a bit of proverbial gasoline on the discussion.

"Boss, the initial stab wound on both girls was perfect for almost immediate incapacitation," said Marianne. She held up a report from the medical examiner, pointed, and read directly. "It was to the left posterior chest near the tenth rib in the intercostal space with penetration of the descending thoracic aorta—that was on both women."

"Very precise," William agreed. He folded his arms and maneuvered his back in the uncomfortable chair.

"And who teaches that?" I asked.

"The military?" said William with a snicker.

I said, "So, smart guy—any specific branch and group? Was this a signature quick kill of any group in particular?"

"I'm thinking specialized strike teams like Rangers, Delta Force, Navy SEALs, Green Berets," said Clark.

"Excuse my ignorance, but do they teach this stuff to normal infantry guys in basic training?" I asked.

"Kind of," replied Marianne, "but they don't really go over and over it to develop this type of precision and accuracy."

William pointed to the medical examiner's report. "It says here, Angela's decapitation was by sharp force between the fourth and fifth vertebrate. I think that adds to the skill and strength."

"Didn't the FBI indicate in their profile that he may have considerable strength?" I asked.

"So, we're looking for a military badass like Rambo?" the Kid said.

"Both of these women were rather athletic and had medium builds. They wouldn't go down without a fight," snapped Clark.

Marianne added, "Yeah, Angela seemed to be a scrapper and didn't take crap from anybody, it looks like from the reports."

"Is there anyone who doesn't think that he was associated with the military or had some type of training?" I asked.

"I'm not so convinced. He could have read up on it in a book or got the training elsewhere," the Kid said.

"Yeah, but reading up on it and doing it to strong and athletic women are entirely different things," Mark said.

"I agree, Mark," said Marianne. "I think he had advanced training."

"Me, too," said William. Dom nodded.

I said, "Okay, Kid, you may indeed be right, and this was self-taught, and who really knows at this point, but maybe we should focus on military backgrounds."

"I think we should sort them out first," interjected Clark. "I think that we should also consider the proximity to Luke Air Force Base. It's not that far a drive from the base in the west part of the valley to the area where the girls were killed."

I nodded in agreement because I already mapped it on the internet, and indeed, it was twenty to twenty-five miles away. "That's a great point, Clark. The only downside is that it might be hard to figure out who was stationed there at the time. I wouldn't think their records would go back that far."

"It's worth looking into," Clark said. "I've got a buddy who is in the office of special investigations in the Air Force. He might have some connections over at Luke."

"Are there any badass ground fighters in the Air Force?" asked Dom, poking fun at the branch.

"I can't think of any, but they may have some specialized fighting groups. Maybe some pilots who have survival training," Mark said.

The Kid looked at his smartphone and said, "It looks like the Air Force may have a special pararescue school, which teaches advanced techniques."

"Marianne? Do you know?" I asked.

"No, but I can check with my NCIS connections."

"Thanks!" I said.

"Okay, guys, as we sift through the files, let's be mindful of military training and put them at the front of the line for DNA collection. Clark, you're going to check with your buddy for information on any connection to Luke Air Force Base. Marianne, you're going to check with NCIS to see if the Air Force has any specialty trained units."

"Yep," said Clark.

"I will this afternoon," said Marianne.

"Thanks, guys!" I said as everyone filed out of the conference room. *The killer was no match for us.*

❧

Mark meandered into my office with a devilish grin and requested to take me on what he referred to as an "enlightening tour." The basement was once a vibrant sector of the headquarters, which was constructed in 1973. Currently, it was a sleepy and deserted skeleton. It accommodated a sad collection of outdated office and vintage computer equipment.

The basement had rooms and veiled closets with, often, old and flickering fluorescent lighting. I shuffled close to Mark like an eight-year-old in a haunted house. We entered a room that housed a vast array of office furniture from the 1980s, and Mark headed to the light switch tucked in a far corner. "They put these switches in the oddest of places," he said.

"Seriously! And why do we keep all this old crap? Why not donate it?"

"Sarge, haven't you learned yet? We're the government. We get to things when we get to things. Sometimes decades later. The room is right here. By the way, you owe me for all this hazardous work."

Mark turned on the light. I was relieved nothing fled from the darkness, but was in disbelief at what looked to be hundreds and hundreds of discolored bankers boxes. I said, "Um, all of these boxes are related to the canal murders?"

"Yeah, I might just be retired by the time we get through all of those."

I shook my head at the volume of information.

"And that's not all of it," Mark blurted out with a smile.

"What do you mean? There's more?" I rubbed my temples.

"Oh, yeah! You see those file cabinets? Those are chock-full of canal stuff. Oh, and upstairs near William's cubicle, there's a four-foot-tall cabinet with all kinds of binders with canal murders, et cetera."

"When do you retire again?" I asked. I desperately wanted to sit down, but the only seats were in the other basement room and saturated with dust. I pulled off a box lid and gaped at the reams of paper.

"So, do you want the good news?"

"Um, yeah, that would be nice, Mark."

"Well, based on my preliminary research, it looks like they did a good job of organizing all this stuff over the past twenty years. Apparently, from all these boxes and this information, they made a comprehensive database with all the tips from citizens, other agencies, and canal contacts."

"That's huge! Can I see that list of the files, please?"

Mark massaged his neck and replied, "Well, I need to do a bit of work on it and collaborate with the computer guys, but I should be able to get it uploaded into Excel."

"You'll have that done by close of the business day, right?" I said with a smile.

Mark laughed, "Well, not quite. I'll see what I can do in the next week or so. Remember, it's still government work—get-to-it-when-we-get-to-it philosophy, Sarge."

⌇

Clark stood with his six-foot-two frame in my office doorway.

"Where do I start? Besides the go-nowhere FBI profiles," Clark said. It was pretty obvious Clark was not a big fan of the federal agency thanks to his dealings with them on his massive serial killer investigation in 2006.

Clark told me they swooped in to effectively take over the investigation and steer it in another direction based on politics. Clark was not motivated by such politics and merely wanted to take down really bad guys and solve crimes for victims and their families. Clark's no-nonsense direction based on years of boots-on-the-ground street experience and grit ultimately broke the case and terminated the killer's wanton crime spree.

"Read the reports for both Angela and Melanie. Marianne and William will obtain DNA from the names in the original reports. Mark will provide organization. With your background, do you want to help me with the files? Mark is putting together a list from the files with all the names of potential leads collected over the years. Let's go see where he's at on it."

Clark and I straddled piles of papers near Mark's cubicle.

"I know what you're thinking, Sarge."

"Still cluttered."

"Cluttered but organized!" He looked at his computer. "I managed to get it all loaded into a spreadsheet, sorted and tabbed. I think it turned out pretty good, given there's almost a thousand entries."

"The names in the files came from tips that flowed in over the years from officers, other law enforcement agencies around the country, and citizens. Is that right?"

"Right. You see, I *am* organized," Mark said.

"You did a phenomenal job, as usual. However, I think we might be dead before we get through all these creepy bastards."

"Yeah, I'm not sure how to do it. You've got the stripes, though. Good night." He cackled as he headed for the door.

I looked at Clark. "Just you and me to sift through these massive files. Thoughts on dividing the names?"

"I say we divide it in half. How about I start from *A* and work forward? You take *Z* and work backward. We'll eventually try to meet in the middle near *M*." Looking back, we should have started in the middle.

"I like it! All we can do is try, right?"

"Yep."

"From my cursory research, it appears prior detectives did workups on the information. However, they probably didn't get DNA on the creeps because most of these tips and contacts came in during the few years after the murders, before DNA really got going in the late 1990s."

Clark said, "So, we're going to have to prioritize the really good ones to go and get their DNA?"

"That seems like as good a plan as any."

❧

For the next few weeks, I sifted through the creepy canal list, working backward, during every spare chance away from my mundane supervisory and other daily duties. The entries ranged from noteworthy and helpful to outright bizarre to downright silly. It seemed like everyone called in to give their two cents.

A sample:

- Caller works at Dillard's Travel Agency 1700 to 2100 at Metrocenter. Both subjects were in her office Monday night talking about the killing. Both had alcohol on their breath. One stated to the other, "We couldn't have been that 'fucked' up last night . . ."
- Caller was walking her dog Sunday, 11-8-92, at approx. 10:15 A.M. when she observed two men shoveling sand into a box in the bed of the listed pickup along the bike path 25th Avenue south of Thunderbird. She cannot ID.
- Writer felt the murder of Angela sounded like a ritual practice carried out by an Indian tribe in the East. Feels the murderer is a religious crazy who is an Indian or someone that converted to their beliefs.

- Retired detective. Giving his opinion on what to look for or who to check out. Feels we should look at Burmese, Laos, Thailand Triangle Cult.
- The caller had a dream, the spirit whispered "tattoo." The caller saw a bouquet of black dahlias.
- Psychic said she saw a vision of the above suspect. She would not leave her info because she was afraid officers would contact her for tips on the lottery.
- Met someone who had scriptures, said they were evil. Made remarks about cutting off heads. Wants to be called to give info to detective.
- Subject has headless barbie dolls in his closet with his wife's name on them.
- Caller said he was drinking in Wayne's Bar, Northern & Freeway, on evening of 1-4-92. He heard "Bob" say, "If a woman spits my load out, I'd cut the bitch's head off." It is possible that "Bob" is a regular customer in the bar.

And the list went on and on. Yet, even with the bizarre and silly ones, one thing resonated loudly. There was no shortage of creepy men out there.

ↄ

Mark hollered at me from his cubicle when I walked by. "So, I may not have a PhD like William, but I was thinking about something rather obvious in the reports. Did anyone ever rule out the Fisher King?" Mark was a very methodical and old school style detective.

Mark Qualls, the so-called Fisher King, found Angela's head in 1992, several days after the murder. When original investigators interviewed him, he was drunk and appeared incapable of such a level of violence. They obtained a blood sample from him in the 1990s, but there was no indication he had been ruled out by DNA comparison.

"I didn't see anything. Those lab reports are hard to read."

"Do you mind if I call over to Kelley and make sure?" Mark asked.

"Yes, of course. I can't believe I didn't think to make sure he had been excluded. He definitely knew the area and liked the canals. He took off after inserting himself into the investigation. If you're right, you could be field promoted and take my job."

He laughed. "I don't want your headaches, but it would be nice to solve it sooner than later."

෴

Mark came into my office the following week and told me he had spoken to Kelley. She researched the lab reports and found that the Fisher King was not a match to our unknown killer.

"Too easy, but glad he wasn't overlooked," Mark said. Mark took things in stride.

Strike one.

CHAPTER 8
THE CHURCH AND THE PROFESSOR

I sat alone with no distractions in the parking lot. Something specific was troubling me from the original reports. I had to follow my gut and check it out. I read supplement 63 for something like the tenth time. A couple who lived at Angela's complex went out for a walk on the night of the murder between midnight and 1 A.M. They were headed to the Circle K when they saw a suspicious person walk by the complex. This person walked eastbound on the north side of Cactus Road and appeared nervous. He looked back at them and all around the area, and he appeared to be holding something under his jacket with both hands.

The couple described him as a white male, about five-ten, thirty to thirty-five years old, with a thin build and blondish-brown hair. The man wore beige pants, a white shirt, and a dark beige jacket. He had thick or big brown-framed glasses and wore loafers.

I wrote at the bottom of the supplement: "glasses—the graffiti on the tunnel walls from Melanie's murder. Man with glasses in the fedora hat with a presumed trench coat. What did he carry?" It was hard to write my next thought. It was horrid. I pushed through the feelings and wrote "Angela's head?"

Supplement 82 followed in my file folder. Supplement 82 described another unrelated couple who came forward with information about what they saw on Sunday evening at about 6:45 P.M. This couple lived near Angela's complex and went to walk their dog at the park north of Cactus

Road near 25th Avenue. They told officers that at about 7 to 7:05 P.M. they saw a white woman who matched Angela's description riding a mountain bike from the north side of the park southbound toward them. She rode at a fast pace but slowed to avoid hitting their dog. She appeared to check her watch, and then rode westbound on the north side of Cactus Road.

The couple walked to the north side of the park and hung out for another twenty minutes or so, and then walked eastbound past a church located at 2340 West Cactus. They saw a man check the church's outer doors with his left hand. He carried something in the other hand, but the couple could not tell what this item was. Once he saw them, he walked to the other side of the church and kept looking over his shoulder. The church was totally dark, and no cars were in the parking lot. They thought maybe the guy was the church caretaker.

I looked back at supplement 63. I wondered if the descriptions matched. Kind of: late thirties to early forties, white guy, five-eight, 160 pounds, with short, blondish hair. He wore a white or cream-colored T-shirt underneath a tattered sweater. There was nothing noted about glasses on this man.

Is there a possible connection to that church? The killer used the church or grounds to stash the head? Was he truly a caretaker? Did he belong there? Was this a big coincidence? A transient just pulling on doors? There's so much religious symbolism in the murders, or at least Melanie's, that I think it's worth checking out.

I pulled my car into the parking lot of the Lutheran Church of the Master. The wooden doors on the church were ornamentally etched and crafted of strong oak. I walked into the main foyer area and saw a friendly-looking, late-middle-aged man seated at a desk. "Can I help you?" the man said.

"Yes, I am a detective with Phoenix PD and just wanted to ask you a few questions."

He extended his hand and said, "Nice to meet you. I'm Roger. I'm a deacon here and volunteer as church staff."

"I work in cold case homicide, and I am working two cases from the early 1990s. This church was in existence and under the same name back then, correct?"

"Yes, it was indeed. My wife and I joined this church in the 1980s and have been here ever since."

"Wow! That's incredible," I said. "Do you, by chance, remember the young woman who was murdered just south of here near the apartment complex on the bike trail in 1992?"

"Yes, I do. It was all over the news at the time. It sent shockwaves through the community, not to mention making our congregation fearful that something so bad could happen so close."

"Do you remember if the police came here to the church?" I asked.

"Yes, I vaguely remember them coming and asking questions. Unfortunately, nobody knew anything. It happened at night, and there was no one at the church."

"Did you have any type of church caretaker or janitor who would come here at night or stay here?" I asked.

"No, we've never had anyone like that."

"It's a long time ago, I understand, but do you remember who would have access to the church after hours?"

"Well, I don't remember specifically, but I would say the head pastor, the associate pastor, and other deacons. It's hard to say, unfortunately, because we didn't have a great tracking system in place until recently."

"I'm going to read you a description of a man seen hanging around this church that night. White male, late thirties to early forties, thin build, five-foot-eight-inches tall, blond hair. Does it sound familiar, by any chance?"

Roger shook his head. "No. Over the years we have had a lot of transients try and get in. We had a homeless guy break in recently just to sleep."

"Yeah, unfortunately, along the interstate there seems to be a lot of transient activity. Okay, what about the pastors and the deacons?" I asked.

"I can't remember the deacons, but I will write down the names of the pastors for you." He wrote down two names on one of his business cards. "This one retired shortly after those murders and is now living in a care facility in Sun City. The other arrived here in the early 1990s, if I remember correctly, and left in the mid-2000s. There were some issues with him. I can't remember exactly when. I think my wife has all the old church directories at our home. I can see if we can dig those out for you to look through."

"If it's not a huge trouble, that would be much appreciated," I said.

"Okay, I'll ask her tonight and get back to you in the next few days."

"Oh, Roger, one more thing—does the church have a basement?"

"No. No basement. We've expanded over the years and added some buildings for Sunday school." He pointed these out as we walked out the front door.

"And when were they added?"

"2005 or so."

ح

When I got back to the office, I did a work-up on the pastors Roger wrote down. The senior pastor, who lived in Sun City, would have been in his fifties at the time of these murders. He had a clean record and didn't match the description given by either couple of the subject lurking around the church that night. I toggled to the associate pastor. He started at the church in April 1992. Angela was killed in November 1992. *Kind of strange.*

Roger called. He told me that they did in fact have several old church directories from that time. He told me I could come by his house to look at them.

"Roger, before I let you go, I do have one more question. You mentioned that the associate pastor left the church under bad circumstances. Can you share more on this?"

"There were some financial issues that we were concerned with. Nothing too crazy."

☙

I met Roger and his wife at their house in Scottsdale. The house was a modern Pueblo-style ranch. The front yard consisted of desert landscaping: large boulders complemented with sporadic cactuses and succulents.

"So, here is a directory with photos from 1990 and ones from 1993, 1994, and 1995. I couldn't find one from 1991 or 1992, unfortunately," Roger said.

I was looking for a needle in a haystack, I thought. *But what if he was there somewhere?* I had to look. I had to follow this possible connection and be thorough.

"Roger, were there any members that you can think of from back then that were a bit strange? I know it's a strange question, and I'm not trying to put you in an awkward position."

"Not really. There were always some different kinds of churchgoers, but no one that I can think of that acted crazy or capable of this level of violence."

I wrote down the names of the three who matched the description. One, in particular, looked creepy. I know I'm not supposed to pass judgment by looks alone, but there was something with his eyes.

After Roger's house, I drove over to the associate pastor's house. I heard two men talking loudly inside. I rang the doorbell, and a young man in his early twenties answered the door. I saw a man who matched the pastor's picture in the distance, trying to hide behind a pillar.

I asked for the pastor. The young man seemed rattled and then said, "Just a moment, Detective."

In a few seconds, the pastor came out and said, "Can I help you?"

"Yes, sir, I'm Troy. I work with Phoenix PD Cold Case Homicide. It was a long time ago, but do you remember hearing about the young woman who was murdered while she was biking just south of your church on Cactus?"

"No, not really. I do remember they found some girl in a canal south of there in, say, 1993."

"We spoke with a deacon, Roger, who said that your church was visited by police in 1992, and your congregation was fearful as it was a very violent murder that happened so close to the church."

"Oh, yeah, I know Roger."

"So, you don't remember the 1992 murder closer to your church?"

"I can't say that I do."

"Did you have a caretaker or anyone who went to the church after hours?"

"Not that I recall."

I used an envelope ruse to obtain his DNA. This is when the target, in this case the pastor, is asked to look at a series of photos from an open envelope. Random jail photos of known local thieves are placed in the stack. The target is then to place the photos back inside and seal the envelope. The saliva provides a good clean sample for the lab to work with. I felt bad even entertaining thoughts of a pastor being our killer. Yet, there have been men of the cloth who have done bad things before. It's the perfect disguise to hide behind.

❧

I got the call from Kelley at the lab a few weeks later, and she told me that the pastor was eliminated. *Well, I had to try.*

I did workups on the three creepy-looking fellows from the church registry. Two of them had extremely clean records. However, the one who looked the creepiest had some minor run-ins with the law and lived by himself. Since he matched the description given by the couple, I decided to pursue it. I went out to his house and explained that I was looking into two murders from the early 1990s. I asked him if he was a deacon at that time.

"No, sir. I was never a deacon."

"So, you never had a key?"

"No," he said.

"Did you ever go to the church after hours to pray, et cetera?"

"No, sir. I went on Sundays for service, and that's it."

"Okay, do you remember any strange people hanging out around the church?"

"No, but there are a lot of homeless people in that area."

I obtained his DNA with an envelope ruse and left. *Maybe I'll get lucky.*

❧

A couple of weeks passed. Kelley called me and said that guy was ruled out also. I sighed. *The church connection is a dead end for now. I had to look into it, though.*

❧

Professor Herbert Brooks lived with his elderly father in a run-down shack in a remote area of Maryland. When Marianne knocked on the door along with a county sheriff, he answered with a look of shock. He seemed rattled, his hands trembled, and he stuttered in response to their preliminary questions. It was hard for Marianne to believe he was once a polished professor at a university in California. He also had held the high rank of major in the Army's special forces.

We learned from the report that our first victim, Angela, was his faculty assistant while going to DeVry in Los Angeles. Angela had been on a business trip to California just prior to returning to Phoenix, and she visited Brooks at his trailer outside of Los Angeles. At that time, he told the original detectives he had no romantic interest in her. He added, though, that she struck him as a "twenty- or twenty-one-year-old virgin." When asked to clarify, he said he didn't know that, but that was his "initial impression." He then got very upset and told detectives that everyone around him was dying. He regained his composure and told them about his time with her the week prior to her murder. They had dinner and drinks that night. Brooks told her to end the relationship with her boyfriend. She told him that they were living apart. They went into his RV for a while. Then he told detectives he gave her a "lingering hug."

Marianne found his statements odd. Mark also found Brooks in the files. An anonymous caller indicated that he gets upset and starts yelling every time someone brings up Angela's murder. He looked like a great lead, but we couldn't find any connection to Melanie. Of course, he could have been more random after an attack on Angela, whom he knew.

In the Maryland shack, Marianne saw a machete behind the door. During their long interview, he admitted to knowing Angela but claimed it was purely platonic. He denied any involvement whatsoever in her murder. His nervous demeanor persisted throughout the interview. Unfortunately, there was not enough probable cause to make an arrest without DNA confirmation, so she obtained a DNA swab and returned to Phoenix.

❧

Marianne jetted into my office and said, "Boss, I'm really excited about this Brooks guy."

Startled, I said, "Does he have a nickname, like William likes to use? Puppet's brother, Joker, Fozzy?" I liked to keep things light given the brutality of what we dealt with every day.

"I don't know. The Professor. Does that work?"

"Yes, rather boring compared to William's stellar nicknames, but that works. Kelley has the DNA sample, right?"

"Yes, now, we just wait. He was so weird, though—the lingering hug, the virgin comment, the machete, special forces. It all adds up."

"Not to mention Marianne said he was nervous as could be," said William, as he appeared and grabbed the doorframe. The patented back stretching was next. He groaned.

"To think that he was in the report the whole time. Mind boggling!" I said.

"I don't want to get disappointed, boss. This guy looks good. I pray to the Lord it's him, and we can give some peace to Angela's and Melanie's families," Marianne said.

I knew Marianne was a devout Christian. She embodied every rule in the biblical commandments, for sure. She would have donated her entire paycheck to the sick and poor, if she hadn't needed to keep her land and feed her horses.

"I would bet a case of Diet Cokes on it," said William.

"That stuff is killing you, William," I said. "You need to drink more straight-up water in the desert." William loved multiple Diet Cokes at work and beer, responsibly, off-duty. Water was contained therein, according to William.

"Okay, I'm gonna get back to writing this performance rating for Mark."

"Boss, tell him to clean up his cubicle in there," Marianne said and laughed.

"Somehow he's the epitome of organization," I said.

❧

A few weeks flew by and Kelley called. We caught up with our significant others, parents, and dogs, as usual. Then she broke the bad news: Brooks had been ruled out of the investigation by DNA. I was disappointed, to say the least, but even more disappointed to have to tell Marianne and William. They took it in stride. William responded with a joke. He didn't let much bother him. Marianne seemed sad, her hopes smashed, but she was a very positive person. She said, "I have faith. On to the next one, boss. We'll find our killer."

Keep going.

CHAPTER 9
THE CLERK, THE HEADHUNTER, AND THE MEDICAL SCIENTIST

The local authorities in West Virginia knocked on the trailer door. Marianne was directly behind them. A washed-up man finally answered the door with a what-do-you-want look on his face. It was obvious he had a strong dislike for police in any shape or form. The officers told the man he was not under arrest, but they had a court order to get his DNA. They introduced him to Marianne. Roy Lyons seemed rattled by this intrusion.

Lyons was listed in the original report. He was a Circle K clerk who tried to sell a bike at his work at 27th Avenue and Deer Valley right after Angela's murder in 1992. An anonymous male called the US Marshals and told them about the bike. The anonymous male later called back to say that Lyons buried the head across the field from the apartment complex. The original detectives tracked down Lyons, but he refused to talk to them. They put him under surveillance but found nothing unusual.

Right after Melanie's murder in 1993, someone called in and said that they overheard a Circle K clerk telling a boy that he had a bike he wanted to sell. The original detectives believed Lyons was the same clerk. Lyons had an extensive rap sheet with a clear pattern of deviant sexual behavior, violence toward women, substance abuse, and possible mental illness. He also had served in the Army in Vietnam, according to sources.

Lyons was interviewed by Marianne in West Virginia. He denied knowing either Angela or Melanie, but he failed the polygraph. Our hopes were high on this one.

∾

Dom's cubicle was a few steps outside my office. I walked toward him as he was in the middle of telling a joke to a group of officers. I had to laugh. He was the court jester, but somehow, he got all of his work done and then some.

He said, "Boss, Marianne thinks Lyons is the canal killer."

Marianne poked her head out from her cubicle down the row. "That's not what I said, Dom! I just think he looks good."

"He's got quite the criminal history to back the theory. He also appears to be written up in both murders," I said.

"Marianne just wants to show us all up. *Look at me, I'm Marianne, I solved the canal murders all by myself, look at me,*" he said. He loved to tease Marianne, and we all knew she enjoyed the banter. The subject matter was too heavy not to have a joker like the self-titled Dominator.

"The proof will be in the DNA," I said and walked away. *Lyons could definitely be our killer.*

∾

Several agonizing weeks later, Kelley called me. I sat upright. I braced for good news, but only bad news followed. She told me Lyons had been ruled out also. I got up and put a line through Lyons's name on my dry erase board. Qualls and Brooks also had strikes through their names. Marianne and William took the news again in stride. William just popped another Diet Coke and said, "On to the next," while Marianne told me she had continued faith we would find our killer. *Another strike. Keep going.*

It was odd. A man listed in the original reports told officers he had been out trying to find the head and her bike after Angela's murder in 1992. The man, Thomas Kaiser, reported finding a bag with a knife under a tree near the TGI Friday's restaurant a few days after Angela's murder. Angela and Joe, her fiancé, had eaten lunch there on the Sunday afternoon before her death, and it was somewhat close to where her head was found in the canal.

"Who does that? Can you imagine telling your wife, 'Hey, honey, I'm gonna go look for a head. It's all good, sweetheart. Just being a good citizen,'" JJ said, oozing with his usual sarcasm. "I mean, come on!"

"What do you think, Clark?" I asked.

"It's definitely strange. I don't think any of us can understand that level of citizen assistance. He needs to be ruled out, regardless." Clark feathered his hair with his hands. I knew he did this when he concentrated. He had a boatload of experience and took down two serial killers in the mid-2000s. His opinion carried great weight with me.

We discussed the fact that our lab looked at that knife in the 1990s and found no blood on the blade, handle, or sheath. Also, there were no prints on the knife. Clark and JJ located Kaiser in the Phoenix area, and he volunteered to give them his DNA sample. Whispers of Kaiser possibly being the canal killer floated around our workspace. *Pins and needles again,* I thought. *Could it be?*

A few weeks went by, and Kelley called over from the lab. Another left jab to the face: She told me Kaiser was also ruled out. I half-heartedly joked that I was gonna start calling her the Lead Killer.

She laughed and said, "I've said it before. That's the only way you're gonna solve these murders is by giving us samples."

I crossed off Kaiser's name on the board and went to tell JJ. His cubicle bulged with family photos and Michigan State paraphernalia. His young son was decked out in every Michigan State outfit imaginable.

"JJ, Kaiser's out," I said.

JJ tossed his paperwork aside and said, "That's great! My boy has a basketball game tonight, and I really didn't have time to make a massive arrest."

He wanted to solve the murders as bad as anyone else on the team; he just handled things with overt sarcasm.

Clark had gone home for the day. He cussed for a solid five minutes when I told him the next day.

✑

Dom strolled into my office. He asked me about the bull stock market. We were both finance dorks and believed in the power of long-term investments.

"How about this Tobias cat?" asked Dom.

"The medical scientist?" I asked. I had read the reports multiple times but neglected to add him to our lead list.

John Tobias was a name that surfaced during the aftermath of the murders. He was the subject of an FBI notice that possibly matched our murders to one in France. Tobias was a medical scientist who spent some time overseas. The French government issued a warrant, according to the FBI, for a heinous mutilation murder of a young French girl.

"Yeah, we rule him out yet?" asked Dom.

"I don't think so. Can you work that?"

"Yo, the Dominator is on it," Dom said, and he strolled back to his cubicle. He yelled out to no one in particular, "Dom is on the case! Gonna solve the canal murders. It's gonna happen."

✑

Later that day, Dom darted into my office in a move Marianne would be proud of. I could tell he was propelled by excitement. He launched past the normal finance talk and jokes and told me the local police in Florida helped us get Tobias's DNA sample. Dom said, "They literally just knocked on the door and said we needed it. They said he was not upset—in fact, he was very cooperative. I wish they all were that easy."

"You think he's our guy?" I asked.

"He mutilated the French girl, right? Get ready to put my face all over the news, Sergeant Hillman! I'm gonna go big time for blowing this thing wide open!"

"We. You mean the team blew this wide open."

"Yeah, we'll probably get you and Marianne a few minutes of airtime out of my hour." I knew Dom was not about the glory. He had a teenage daughter and was horrified at what happened to Angela and Melanie. His humor was his shield.

∾

Kelley called. I joked that I was going to stop taking her calls. She told me Tobias was out also. *Can't we catch a break? Rinse, lather, repeat.* I crossed out the name on the board. I found Dom among a group of detectives telling a funny war story from his days in Maryvale Precinct.

"Boss, what's happening?"

"Don't order your tuxedo for the awards ceremony yet, Dominator."

"Tobias, too? Seriously?"

"Yup, sorry."

He motioned with his hands. "That's me dropping the microphone and walking off stage. This is getting ridiculous."

"Keep going." I was trying to stay positive. But with all the recent strike-outs, it was hard to keep disappointment at bay.

CHAPTER 10
THE CONNECTIONS
AND THE CYBERSTALKER

M y wife, Karyn, went out with her nursing girlfriends to Old Town Scottsdale for a much-needed stress-neutralizing night away from dealing with the compassion fatigue of hospital shift work. I grabbed a six-pack of a local brewery's beer and went to one of the spare bedrooms of our home that had been converted to an office, which, unbeknownst to me at the time, was earmarked to become a nursery. I took out a notepad and started a deep dive into all things on the internet, writing on the top of the notepad "Connections / Possible Related Cases."

The killer could be in our reports or our files. But what if he wasn't? One of the things that really bothered me about our two murders was that they were both high profile and horrific murders, and we couldn't find what led up to the killer's actions with Angela and what followed his actions with Melanie. *The death of the perpetrator is the easy way out, and maybe that's what happened.*

I ran across an article that gripped me and wrote on my notepad: "(1) Diana Vicari, 19-year-old girl, Tucson, AZ, October 22, 1992." The article said she went to a rock concert and was found in a dumpster downtown. Her arms were discovered in the dumpster, severed below the shoulders and wrapped in trash bags. The rest of the body was never found. Tucson PD arrested Lemuel Prion and charged him with the murder in 1997. This maggot bragged about taking a woman into the desert, sexually assaulting her, killing her, and cutting her up. Investigators discovered in late 1992 that he had kidnapped a girl, taken her to a secluded area, and threatened her with a knife. She survived, and Prion was convicted in 1999. The court overturned the case in 2003, and he was set free because prosecutors failed to show evidence that there was another suspect, John Mazure. There was no evidence tying either man to the murder of Diana Vicari.[1] I jotted down in the notepad, "Looks like case unsolved????? Same age group, time frame very close to Angela's, significant cutting/mutilation of victim, AF Base in Tucson."

I took a sip of beer and found an article about a girl named Jennifer Pentilla, who was listed as a cold case in New Mexico. She was last heard from on October 17, 1991, when she was biking across the Western US from San Diego. Her Bible, tent, clothing, and other items were left beneath a bush. Her bike and some other personal belongings were never found, which piqued my interest. *Angela's and Melanie's bikes weren't found, either.* The article indicated that Jennifer took a bus from Phoenix to Tucson.[2] *Interesting.* I put down the following on my notepad attaching the article: "(2) Jennifer Padilla: time frame matches, victim rode bike, bike taken by perp, religious, connection to Arizona."

I ran across another article regarding the 1984 death of Claire Hough in San Diego. She was fourteen years old and had her throat cut and left breast cut off at a place called Torrey Pines State Beach. In October 2014, San Diego PD arrested a San Diego crime lab technician named Kevin Charles Brown.[3] After reading some more in various articles on the perp, I wrote down "(3) Claire Hough: connection to water, throat slashed, cutting, perp lab tech meets our church description, used van and stun gun, sand pushed in mouth—discuss with team and can we compare DNA?"

I rubbed my eyes and found another article titled "El Dorado–Sutter Decapitation Murders," which discussed a murder of a nineteen-year-old woman named Veronica Martinez. According to the article, she went missing on January 27, 1992, and was found two months later in a ravine off a highway. She was decapitated.[4] I wrote: "(4) Veronica Martinez:

similar age to our victims, CA nearby, same time frame, decapitation same as Angela." The article described another woman found partially buried in Sutter County, California, on June 13, 1996. She was decapitated and her hands were removed and never found. I scrawled "same time frame, decapitation, same age range of victim, CA nearby, decapitation and hands removed—different but connected?"

I needed a break, but I couldn't stop and found an article about three unsolved murders in Yavapai County just north of Phoenix which is in Maricopa County. The article read, "Cathy Sposito, 23, was murdered on June 13, 1987, while hiking on the Thumb Butte Trail west of Prescott. The body of Pamela Pitt, 19, was found September 29, 1988, adjacent to Alto Pit, a popular party site in Prescott." Another article said Sposito was last seen riding a mountain bike and that she was beaten to death.[5] I wrote: "(5) Cathy Sposito & Pamela Pitt—same age range of victim, proximity to Phoenix, prior to our murders so maybe getting more violent, victim on bike on trail."

Just a few more. I found an article titled "Swedish Nanny Murder."[6] According to the article, on June 23, 1996, a twenty-year-old woman named Karina Holmer disappeared outside a Boston nightclub. Later that next day, authorities found her severed upper body in a dumpster. The article said that she was cut in half with "surgical precision." The case has never been solved. I wrote down "Karina Holmer—same age, blonde, cut in half like Angela, 22 miles from Air Force base."

I found another case in Pima County, which is south of Phoenix. The bulletin on the Pima County sheriff's website listed that Joan Archer was killed on April 27, 1986. She was supposed to attend a seminar in Phoenix but never made it. Her bicycle was missing and later found next to a nearby road. In July 1986, citizens found a lower leg with the sneaker still on in a wash. Her entire remains were found in late July, just east of that wash. The medical examiner ruled that she died from multiple stab wounds.[7] Further research indicated the sheriff listed a Stephen Skaggs as a strong person of interest. When I looked more closely at Skaggs, I learned that he had been stationed at Luke Air Force Base in the 1970s and committed a rape. I wrote down "Joan Archer—same victim age range, bicycle involved, sneaker still on matching our victims, near a wash/water, possible Air Force connection with Skaggs, Skaggs in CODIS database?"

I was a madman of a sort and couldn't quit the tear I was on. I squinted at the glowing screen in my office and found yet another bulletin from Pima County Sheriff's Department, which read:

> December 10, 1998, a security guard on patrol near the canal found a deceased female in the area known as Three Ponds. The victim was found nude except for socks on her feet and her top pushed up around her neck. The autopsy revealed the victim suffered a very violent death which included blunt force trauma. Native tree branches were used to penetrate the victim's torso. No evidence of sexual assault was noted.

There was more of interest in the bulletin: "pieces of wood were placed on the chest in the design of a cross or *X*."[8] I wrote down "Jane Doe—socks on feet like our victims, nude, near canal/water, tree branches into torso some kind of symbology, cross on chest."

My hand ached, and my notepad was riddled with notes. I needed a break as much as a strong dose of encouragement that I was headed down the right path. I felt absolutely lost in maggot land. Even though my research kept resulting in more and more questions and was filling a host of beaten notepads, I kept at it in my downtime at work. There *had* to be a connection. Our killer had to have moved on from Phoenix after and been somewhere before. We just weren't seeing it.

Karyn often asked me how disturbing this kind of research was, and I would calmly reply "very," and smile. Then, I would throw back a "Yet it's dreadfully fascinating." She would just shake her head and smile, knowing deep down that I was hopelessly driven and these cases haunted me to my core.

With all this compiled information, I decided to embrace my inner nerdy accountant once more and create a spreadsheet on all these possibly related murders. I was hoping that they would help me find a visual link—the missing object in the photo. I prepared a working timeline of these possibly related murders. The timeline was massive, and my working copy had all kinds of added notes and details. Like a mad scientist, I hung it above my dry erase board and sat back in my creaky chair rocking and squeezed my trusty stress ball. There were so many dead women, and law enforcement in Phoenix and around the country had absolutely no answers.

And to think my wife and I want to bring an innocent child into this awful world.

✑

William knocked on my office door while I was buried in the computer screen. "Boss man, do you have a minute? It's about a development in the canal murders."

"Absolutely. Come on in." I was all ears. We had been at this investigation for almost two years now.

"So, I got a rather strange call from a woman last week wanting to meet with us regarding some possible information on our canal murders. Marianne and I met with her yesterday."

"Okay."

"She said there's some guy named Smith who has been cyberstalking her for the past couple of years. It all started when she was on a dating website. According to her, this guy seemed nice and rather harmless, so they began chatting over the internet."

"Okay."

"Progressively, this Chuck Smith fellow has become 'really weird,' as she put it. He claims that she is not who she says she is and is really his ex-girlfriend from the early 1990s named 'Angie.' He goes further and says that they have a baby girl together, and she has kept the baby girl away from him all these years."

"Interesting. He sounds like a screwball," I said.

William nodded. "She's reported Smith to the dating site over and over, but he keeps coming back with different screen names and ranting about how she could have done that to him, et cetera."

"How does this involve our victims?"

"I'm getting there," William said. "So, over the past month, he has been going into graphic detail talking about how he was there and saw Angela getting attacked and killed."

"Wow! Did he just watch or participate?" I asked.

"She wasn't quite sure, but he puts himself at the scene and gave her a ton of details. She's a smart lady and printed out all the correspondence. Marianne and I are going through it to see for sure."

"Interesting! He inserted himself into the investigation, but years later and in a strange manner," I said.

"Yup," said William. "We'll give you more once we're done going through this stack of emails."

ॐ

The next day William and Marianne came into my office. In typical Marianne fashion, she jetted in first and abruptly said, "This guy looks really good for it, Boss."

"Can you preface what you're talking about?" I asked.

"Boss, come on, our latest creepy guy on the canal murders—Chuck Smith."

"So," William added, "we read through all the emails. He's a nut, but he goes into some detail that was, well, rather disturbing."

"Do tell."

"Well, in one part he claims that he was walking on the bike path the night of Angela's murder in 1992 and saw Angela on the ground. A 'scary' guy in a trench coat with a long machete-like knife approached him. The guy gave him the knife and made him stab her, though he didn't want to. The guy made him masturbate there, too."

"Wait, wait," I interjected. "Made him masturbate?"

William smiled. "I'm only reading what he wrote. It's not out of the realm of possibilities, though."

I shook my head. "It's just a bit farfetched."

"I agree, but he's got a lot of detail in here to suggest he was there. His degree of participation and the man in the trench coat are other matters."

My mind flashed back to the clue painted on the tunnel wall that was discovered after Melanie's murder in 1993—the man in the fedora, which typically goes with a trench coat. "What we don't know," I said, "is how much information was released to the public over the years on these two cases. He may just be regurgitating what he's read. That's concerning to me."

William said, "I think we have enough based on all of this to bring Chuck in here and get his DNA."

I said, "I agree. We need to rule his ass out and figure out how he knows all this stuff."

"He might have been involved. It's just so weird," said Marianne.

"He could be just some wingnut who read stuff and created a fantasy," said William.

The detectives had anticipated my questions for Chuck. He graduated from culinary school. *Good with knives.* He was very religious, his mother was a psychologist, and his stepfather was very abusive. He was also really into astrology. Chuck had hit several points on the FBI profile. William told me Chuck lived in a suburb of Phoenix called Surprise.

"Okay, write the warrant and I'll brief the LT. We're probably going to have the SAU team make the entry on the house." SAU was the Special Assignments Unit, what we called our SWAT team.

✣

At a staging area, I found myself front and center of three large squads of intimidating SAU team officers. My introverted CPA-side kicked in. I stumbled on my first few words and fumbled with my paperwork. I settled down and managed to get the information out on the murders and how we got to Chuck Smith as our potential suspect. Three beefy squads seemed a bit of overkill for one guy with a rather clean criminal background, but I knew a lot of these officers had been on the department for years and vividly recalled these murders. Many even canvassed the canal banks for days, looking for clues. To put it mildly, they all seemed enthusiastic to get the monster who did this to Angela and Melanie.

I got the call a few minutes later that they made entry and had two juveniles in custody as well as the target, Chuck Smith. The chatter over the radio indicated there was no resistance. I drove with Clark to the scene.

Marianne and William took Chuck back to headquarters for an interview, while the rest of us conducted a search warrant on Chuck's house. I kept my phone nearby in case Marianne or William called me. I could only hope we stumbled onto the canal killer.

Chuck's house was a three-bedroom ranch in the middle of a suburban neighborhood. When I walked in, I hoped to see Angela's and Melanie's bikes. Or maybe their Walkmans. *Too easy.* The main living areas hadn't been cleaned in years and were sparsely furnished, which made our search straightforward. Chuck must not have spent much time in the house. His bedroom was small and could have used a good cleaning, but it didn't have much in it besides a bed, nightstand, and dresser. Much to our disappointment, the only significant findings were an old knife and a Bible, which we photographed and seized.

I didn't get a call while out on the search. *Maybe he confessed to everything, and they are still in there with Chuck?* I could finally stop my obsession with the canal murders. A layup in the basketball world of a sorts.

When I got back to headquarters, I tracked down Marianne and William. I said, "Please tell me he is our killer."

Marianne said, "Maybe, boss. He seems more confused and mentally ill than a cold-blooded killer. He adamantly believes that the woman who reported this to us is really his ex-girlfriend, Angie."

"Yeah, we both walked out of that room thinking he's probably not our guy," added William.

I recognized the years of experience both elite detectives had. They could feel a suspect's guilt in their sleep.

Marianne said, "He told us the same version he wrote in the email. He was there on the night of Angela's murder. He denied killing her but said some other guy with a machete made him masturbate."

"That's just weird. Proof will be in the pudding—his DNA won't lie," I said.

"Yeah, fingers crossed," said William.

"What did you guys do with him?" I asked.

William said, "Told him to knock off cyberstalking that poor woman and put him in touch with his counselor. We also let her know how to get a restraining order."

"Kelley knows that his DNA is coming over?" I asked.

"Yep, boss, we already let her know," Marianne said.

"Great work, guys! Now, we just sit back and wait again."

✑

Mark knocked on my office door. His knock was as easygoing as he was. "Sarge, you got a minute?"

"Sure, what's going on?"

"Anything on Chuck Smith? The rest of the squad is afraid to ask. I told them you knew I could walk off the job and retire any day so you couldn't get mad at me."

With his unique humor, Mark brought smiles to a dark world. I said, "Not a thing. I can't help but think about Chuck myself. He put himself at that scene with tons of details. His story was so unbelievable that it was believable in some respects. I don't know what to think."

"Well, if you hear anything . . ."

෴

A few weeks later Kelley called. Chuck was our most promising lead yet. My feet tapped the ground anxiously. "Lay it on me," I said. Then the right hook caught me in the jaw: Chuck Smith had been ruled out. I threw my stress ball at the dry erase board. *I need a vacation.* I delivered the bad news to the team. Disappointment filled their worlds as it did mine. False confessions were a part of our business, especially on high-profile cases like the canal murders. We all knew that, but it was still difficult to stomach. Chuck's imagination had weaved dangerously into what we knew as facts. Yet, the DNA did not lie. We also knew that Chuck didn't mean to lead us down a rabbit hole. He had mental health issues, and we needed to get him help. The team would move on like they always did, but the valleys in the real-world roller-coaster ride were taking a toll. Not to mention, I could hear the skeptical whispers intensify. The doubters in the building who chattered, "The fools thought it was the crazy guy, Smith! Ha! The real canal killer is dead! Why are they wasting their time? He's dead!"

We could not let the failures consume us. They were just part of our journey. We needed to keep moving forward.

CHAPTER 11
THE MODERN-DAY SHERLOCK HOLMES

Y ou got a minute?" William asked.

"Yes. I'm all ears," I said.

"Have you heard of a group called the Vidocq Society?"

"Nope."

"I hadn't either. One of the mothers on a case of mine from 2001 found them on the internet and wanted me to ask them to look at her son's case. I told her I would discuss it with my bosses. I pulled up their website. It's interesting."

I punched the search into Google and the site popped up. William stood over me and said, "Click on 'history' over here."

"Veritas veritatum—the truth of truths," I read from the site. "That's interesting."

William continued, "They call themselves the modern-day Sherlock Holmes. They are out of Philly and founded by these three guys—one is a high-ranking member of the US Customs Service, one was a psychic forensic sculptor, and the other is a retired prison psychologist from Michigan. It says that they used to have luncheons to debate crimes and mysteries. Over time, they began to focus on unsolved deaths and disappearances."

"Okay," I said. "I'm interested."

William took a few steps back to the doorway to reengage his back stretch. "So, Sarge, it looks like there's even a best-selling book out there about what these guys do." He walked back to my desk and pointed toward the screen. "Click on this link. You see here the book is called *The Murder Room: The Heirs of Sherlock Holmes Gather to Solve the World's Most Perplexing Cold Cases* by an author named Michael Capuzzo."

"Fascinating," I said. Finally my mind shifted to where William was going with this, and we locked eyes.

"I don't think that my case from 2001 will meet their criteria, but what about the canal murders? I'm thinking that they might be able to give us some insight as to what we may have missed or what direction to go. What do you think?"

"I think it's a hell of a good idea. We need to convince the chain of command of the value, but I think I can do that. The new lieutenant is a bit cautious, but he believes in us and our mission," I replied. My prior phenomenal leader, Joe Knott, had recently been promoted and was replaced.

"I've got to hit a case eval meeting, but before I go, do me a favor and click over here on this tab that says 'case acceptance.'" It said, "Our sole purpose is to provide guidance to law enforcement agencies to assist them in solving these homicides. Opinions given by our members are personal and offered in the spirit of cooperation and assistance, based only upon the facts presented, and should not be considered formal or legally binding opinions of the society."

I shook with excitement. "How much is it gonna cost? I know that the bosses are going to want to know that."

William said, "I just knew you were going to ask that, so I called Philly and talked to the coordinator. He said that if they accept our case, then they pay for the flight, hotel, and per diem for two detectives. So, the only cost to the department is our time to go and present the cases."

"Did he say anything about what they wanted from us?"

William replied, "He said a one- to two-page summary of the murders would suffice."

"This is good stuff! I see it as a win-win. Let me discuss it with the lieutenant."

"Thank you," William said before he walked to his cubicle.

I shut the door to my office and researched this group. I wanted to be prepared for anything upper management might throw my way in terms of who these experts were. I found an article on the internet titled "Vidocq Society—the Murder Club."[1] I read with interest: "Homicide is always on the menu at this exclusive dining society where some of the world's greatest crime specialists gather each month to solve the grisly, cold case killings."

The author, Ed Pilkington, wrote, "The assembled gourmands include some of the best detective brains in America and across the globe—public prosecutors, FBI profilers, murder detectives, forensic scientists and artists, psychologists and anthropologists, security consultants and coroners." He continued:

> The Society was founded in 1990 by three acquaintances in crime solving—William Fleisher, Richard Walter, and Frank Bender. Fleisher is a large, avuncular, bearded polygraph expert, who was an FBI special agent and top customs investigator. Walter is one of the world's most respected forensic psychologists specialising in delving into the dark mind of the serial killer. Rake-thin and spiky, he has worked across America, but because of his demeanor, people call him "the Englishman." Bender is an artist, who stumbled into forensic work. He uses pencil and clay to reconstruct facial features of victims and suspects as an aid in identification.

If these guys can't help us, then nobody can, I thought. We started with no ego and still had no ego when it came to this case. We just wanted to solve it to give the victims and their families delayed justice and much needed answers. Besides, I could tell morale was starting to run low, and this might give us a jolt of energy, or at least get us out of the rut we seemed to be in after so many dead ends. And I didn't want it to impact our other casework.

I showed my boss the website and described what they offered. I could tell he liked the idea, but he wanted to ensure the Vidocq Society's legitimacy as an organization. He wanted me to vet them with the FBI.

I contacted a supervisory agent. This agent had nothing but good things to say about them and said that they do have a good success rate in helping local agencies when the bureau is not available.

I went back to my lieutenant on the subject. He was pleased with the positive comments from the FBI, but he wanted more. He wanted to know the cost and confidentiality of our cases. I told him there was nothing we pay out of pocket. Regarding confidentiality, I told him they have on file a signed confidentiality agreement they provide to each presenting law enforcement agency. The agreement states they won't speak of the case to any non-Vidocq member without our written permission. He conditionally approved the request, but he told me he would need upper management's approval.

I asked him, "Since Marianne and William are co–case agents on these murders, I would like them to go and present on Vidocq's dime. However, as you know, I have become slightly obsessed with these cases and think that this would be a phenomenal opportunity. I find this group fascinating. Can I go, too? I will pay for all my expenses with my own personal funds. This looks to be one of the highlights of my career."

The lieutenant said, "I don't see why not. I am good with it. Let me just get the blessing of the higher-ups."

The next day I received permission from the chain of command to move forward. I could also attend on my own dime. William and Marianne went to work and diligently summarized both cases. Now, we just had to wait on a response.

❧

A few weeks had passed since we sent off the formal request to the Vidocq Society when William came into my office with a smile on his face.

"Hey there, boss man. So, we got a letter back from Vidocq, and they have approved our case. We're flying out in October."

"Excellent! That's great news. I think it's an excellent opportunity to interact with the brilliant upper echelon of law enforcement. To me, it's the opportunity of a career. I started reading that book *The Murder Room* about how Vidocq operates, and I'm drinking the Kool-Aid. I will pass it along after I'm done."

"You know I can't read with my PhD—I mean, plain high school diploma."

"You're smarter than half of the guys with advanced degrees walking around."

❧

Marianne and William feverishly worked on a PowerPoint presentation based on the vague and simplified guidelines the society gave us. The Vidocq coordinator told us to walk them through the investigations, and the experts would ask questions. *Simple enough*, I thought. The detectives took me through their presentation and asked for my feedback. It was a chronological account of what happened and what we did over the past twenty-plus years. I was very impressed at the balance between details and getting our point across with a consciousness of the time parameters. *Excellent*, I thought at the time. "Great work, guys," I said.

"We're a little nervous, to tell you the truth, boss," said Marianne.

"Yeah, I'm a little bit, too. Hard to know what they are gonna expect and ask. The list of attendees at other past presentations is a bit intimidating. However, with what you put together here, you will be great!"

"I hope so," said Marianne.

"Besides, I will be there as your back-up in case the intellectuals get unruly and hurl pocket protectors at you," I said.

"Aren't you an accounting dork?" said William. "One of those pocket protectors belongs to you?"

I shook my head and said, "I can't shake the CPA stereotype, can I?"

❧

We had arrived in Philadelphia and believed we were prepared for this brilliant group of crime fighters. We weren't. A man in the audience shouted at my two detectives. He raised his right pointer finger toward the ceiling. "Excuse me for trying to get to the point," he said, "but can you please just show us the pictures?"

I could hear a pin drop in the large dining hall at the historic Union League building in downtown Philadelphia. Marianne, William, and I exchanged looks. We were taken aback. We were only halfway through our PowerPoint, and I could feel the sweat beads run down my back.

Then I recognized this shouting man, a prolific profiler and one of the founders of Vidocq. I remembered reading a telling story about him from years earlier. The people in the small town were outraged with the news of the interrogation of a revered priest. To think that a man of the faith raped and murdered the young girl was absurd. The sheriff had lost his mind. He put too much faith in this so-called profiler from Michigan. However, it didn't take long before the eccentric profiler had the priest in tears. The priest had been hiding in plain sight for years. The townspeople could not understand how the profiler knew it was him.

What they didn't know was the profiler studied his prey carefully. With a solid psychology background, he had interviewed more than 20,000 inmates and 2,500 sexual predators in the Michigan prison system. He unlocked them, studied their similarities and differences, and explored their minds. He applied his knowledge to a crime scene and could explain the killer's thoughts and fantasies. He hunted them with his mind.

His name was Richard Walter. He appeared to be in his late sixties or early seventies. He stood at about five-foot-eleven, was thin, and wore a cold black suit draped over his rather bony body. He shouted in what, I believed, to be an English accent. The infamous profiler shouted again, "Please, the pictures, just show us the damn pictures already."

Wow, I thought, *he may be a big-deal founder of the Vidocq Society and all, but this English fellow is a bit aggressive.*

I got up, hurried to the front, and joined the two overwhelmed detectives. In frantic and whispered consultation, we abandoned the PowerPoint slides and switched to the crime scene photos. I returned to my seat, breathed deeply, and prayed this would satisfy the cantankerous profiler. Unfortunately, the photo collection on each victim was lengthy, and the detectives were rattled and unclear on what exactly he wanted to see.

I felt a deep pit of failure in my stomach. I saw the man shake his head in frustration, sit down quickly, roar at the members at his table, and stab at his cake. He then took an angry sip of afternoon coffee.

Richard stood up again, tossed his cloth napkin, and peered through his glasses at the blockaded Marianne and William. *Here we go,* I thought. *This is not going well.* Richard hollered, "Just get to the victims already! I want to see the *damn* injuries!" At this point, the room was ablaze with whispers and disapproving headshakes at Richard's demands. I grasped the expertise and greatness inside the historic room, but I had no idea the amount of ego-flexing and bickering that went on from time to time among these experts.

I stood up to render aid to Marianne and William and provide another unified front to this attack. I took control of the laptop, and we were able to get to the victim injury photos. A dozen hands popped up. One of the women in the audience introduced herself as a religious and cult expert. She indicated that this may have been the work of a devil worshipper. I saw Richard roll his eyes and poke his cake. Another expert indicated she was a blood spatter expert and asked about directionality and casting. I looked over and saw Richard glaring at his peers and equally at us with arms folded. He had a look of distinct scorn. *Wow! Tough crowd*, I thought.

The meeting was set for an hour. Before we knew it, Richard's cofounder counterpart, William Fleisher, got up and thanked us for our time. Fleisher was a retired customs agent and was quite cordial.

"That's it?" I whispered to William and Marianne.

They shook their heads and looked as confused as I was at the sequence of events. I was fully engulfed by a group of intellectuals. Richard approached, but he did not seem angry or agitated at all. It appears Richard just had an interesting way to get his points across in the meeting. He told me about something he invented and published in academic journals from his interviews called the helix.

My head hurt at this point. I craved a strong cup of coffee to catch up with the information surge balanced with a cold beer to relax the nerves. Likewise, Marianne and William had a large group of experts around them. They gave what William would later call a "shit ton" of input. "Have you considered this?" I overheard one of them say. Then another would say, "What about X?" abruptly followed by "How about Y and Z?"

Marianne and William left promptly to get to the airport and fly back to Phoenix. I was scheduled to fly out in the morning. I had not experienced anything like this before in my life, and it was about to get more interesting. Richard and his faction of experts invited me over to a local bar for happy hour and more intense interrogation. A good deal of the happy hour conversation revolved around this group and what they had been up to in their respective positions and cities. They were from all over the country.

Richard finally looked over at me and said, "Dear boy, I am impressed."

I shook my head in disappointment. "I didn't think that we did that great of a job presenting what you guys actually wanted to see and hear."

"Well, that's beside the point, boy." He cackled. "But, you see, never in all our precious years has the mighty Phoenix Police Department come here and sought out our opinion. We certainly saw a few cases that we believed we could help on, but our sources indicated that Phoenix wouldn't entertain the thought of a group of outsiders, let's just say, meddling in their case."

I replied, "That's interesting. I can't really comment on that, but I can say that we have changed our ways and know that we're out of our league on these investigations. They don't teach us how to catch serial killers in any local police homicide training that I've ever heard of."

"Yes, yes, how right you are!" He shook his head smiling and looking around at his expert ensemble. "You guys are way behind on this one," he said cackling.

Admittedly, Richard's demeaning comments were a bit hard to stomach as I believed the original investigator did a great job on the investigations, and we had also. I got a little irritated and defensive at this point. "Frankly, with all due respect to your expertise, I think that we've done a lot on these cases."

"You've done a lot of routine things that normal detectives do. But you won't solve it this way. You need to understand him," Richard said as he locked eyes with me.

Richard drew two coiled lines on the napkin. He wrote large words in the middle. I studied intently as he wrote "fetishisms," "frotteurism," "dominance-submission," "bondage-discipline," "piquerism," "sadism." Richard then drew a line and pointed to the napkin.

"This is the fantasy continuum, and this side is the reality. Ergo, both sides represent progressive development. This is my helix. You must study it and understand it to understand your killer," Richard said.

"What's down here?" I pointed to the line Richard drew on the napkin.

"Yes, yes, yes," Richard said with zeal as he wrote on the napkin. "That's necrophilia and cannibalism. Not all of them get that far down the helix, but some do."

"And our killer?" I asked.

Richard did not blink as he stared at me, "Aw, yes, yes, methinks he might have indeed made it that far on my helix."

"You think he was a cannibal?"

He pointed to the helix. "Yes."

"Do you think he's dead?"

"That's a good question, but let me just say, I don't think so. These guys will begin to get so far on the helix, say around here," and he drew on the napkin, "and won't leave their victims."

"Won't leave their victims? What do you mean?"

Richard glared at me and belted out, "These killers fully disassemble their victims, dissolve them, bury them." He took a long, awkward pause and said, "Eat them, oh yes, yes."

I was exhausted. I wanted to call my wife, Karyn, hear her beautiful voice. I wanted to digest all this information. However, I could not leave. Detectives never received this type of one-on-one training. I needed to forge on.

Not skipping a beat, Richard told me he had worked with Bob Keppel. I clarified with him that Keppel was the one who interviewed Ted Bundy. Richard told me he and Keppel wrote several manuscripts together over the years. Richard described a classification model for understanding sexual murder. He told me there are four subtypes: power-assertive (PA), power-reassurance (PR), anger-retaliatory (AR), and anger-excitation (AE). With power-assertive and power-reassurance types, rape is planned but murder is not. They both have a power interest. The power-assertive type has increasing aggression with the victim that ensures control. The power-reassurance type acts out fantasy and seeks reassurance from the victim. The anger-retaliatory and anger-excitation types plan both the rape and murder, and both are anger driven. The anger-retaliatory type seeks revenge for their anger toward another person by attacking a symbolic victim. And last, but not least, anger-excitation types engage in prolonged torture, exploitation, and mutilation, which energize their fantasy life.

Richard said, "The anger-excitation subtypes are my favorites because they are a fascinating breed, to say the least. Now, who at this table can tell me what type Phoenix PD has on their hands?"

I replied fearlessly, "Due to the torture and mutilation, I would say the last type. Um, you said anger-excitation, right?"

"Yes, yes, that's right! You have an AE on your hands. Oh, how appealing!" Richard said clapping his hands with joy.

"Interesting," I said nodding, trying to digest all this subtype information and the acronyms.

Richard could tell that I was enthralled and continued. "AEs are the rarest, and your boy shares the company of Ted Bundy and Jeffrey Dahmer. Now, good luck!" he said.

He returned after a smoke break. "He's in your files. Ninety to ninety-five percent of these guys were contacted by detectives during the initial investigation or inserted themselves into it somehow over the years. The numbers don't lie, boy. I say, again, that he's in your files."

"That's great, but our files are literally thousands of tips and documents in boxes and file cabinets." I shook my head in utter frustration.

"All that means is that you've got a lot of work to do," he said. He wrote "He's in your files" on the napkin and underlined it. He then wrote "Pathology Trumps Intellect."

"Okay." I wondered how that fit in with the helix, AEs, and our files.

"You asked us why your boy seemed to deescalate from such a brutal murder with your first girl to less mutilation on your second. Well, methinks that regardless of your killer's intellectual ability or intentions, he lost control, and his pathology and needs trumped his intellect. It was all about his fantasy, too. Clear as mud, dear boy?"

"I think I've got you. That makes a lot of sense."

"Oh, and I will leave you with one more thing. These guys like to use sarcastic ruses. They think that they are smarter than everybody else and look at it as a game. They will deliberately do things to demonstrate their sense of power and attitude towards the rest of us."

He scribbled "sarcastic ruses" on my napkin.

I walked back to the hotel. I thought, *So, our killer is in Richard's helix, he's an AE in Richard and Keppel's categorization of sick puppies, and he's somewhere in our neat and tidy files. Simple enough! Let's go back to Phoenix and make an arrest.*

I stayed awake that night even though I was mentally exhausted and remembered that night in high school after watching *The Silence of the Lambs* and Hannibal Lecter's chilling statement to FBI agent Clarice Starling. He had told her that the killer she sought, Buffalo Bill, was in their files. *It must be true,* I thought. Art imitating life, after all. *Hannibal and Richard both say so. In our files. But where in our files, where? Oh, and is* methinks *even a word? And what about* ergo? *Never heard of it.*

CHAPTER 12
THE INTERNATIONAL CONNECTION

I scrolled through the graphic photos Richard sent me and rubbed my forehead. This was both exciting and overwhelming. He just took our investigation to a possible international level.

Richard had called me the day prior. He told me in the late 1990s he was over in Europe teaching for Interpol. He spoke to a Dutch official and a German one. The Dutch one discussed a murder in the early 1990s of a beautiful young South African girl who had been backpacking near Amsterdam. She was found beheaded and displayed near a heavily forested tunnel in the countryside. Her hands were also removed. They never solved the crime or found her head or hands. The German detective said they had something similar. They found a sex worker along a country road near Dusseldorf with her head and hands cut off. Unlike the Dutch murder, her intestines had been removed and strewn about the scene. The Germans never solved that crime, either. Both detectives described getting strange phone calls from someone claiming to be a high-ranking member, a "general," of the US Air Force wanting to know the status of the investigations.

Richard asked me if we had an Air Force base near Phoenix. I told him that Luke Air Force Base was nearby. Richard believed the Dutch and German murders were like ours and were reasonably close to military bases. He also believed that there was a reason that this "general" called those investigators. He suggested the "general" tried to insert himself into both investigations. Richard reminded me of the sarcastic ruse the AE subtypes like to use. These subtypes believed they were smarter than the majority of the population and especially the police. They would do things like show up at a victim's funeral pretending to be a long-lost family member, or they would take photos arm-in-arm with police at a large charity event. They would all but say, "Here I am, but you are too stupid to catch me." They found their antics very amusing.

I researched the two new murders Richard spoke of and the possible international connection. Thompson was the South African backpacker killed near a wooded tunnel in the Netherlands in 1994. Richard only referred to her by her last name; the European authorities had apparently not conveyed the victim's first name to him, and Richard being Richard was more interested in the scene. After all, the scene was his expertise. The Thompson murder was roughly a year after Melanie's murder in 1993. In addition to her head being cut off and missing from the scene, her hands were also cut off and removed. She had a large incision from her sternum area down to her pubic area. There were two large incisions emanating from her pubic area toward the sides of her legs like the killer may have been contemplating cutting off the legs. The entire cut, from a top view, looked to be in the shape of an arrow. I also noticed three incisions on both of her breasts. She was positioned by her killer with her legs and feet over a curb. Her torso and arms rested on a walking/bike path. I wrote down "tunnel" and "bike path" on my notepad.

I researched the second victim, Dittmer, from Germany around 1996. Like Thompson, she was headless, and her hands were cut off. Neither were found at the scene. However, her heart was removed, and her killer placed it between her legs. She, too, had a large vertical incision from her sternum to her pubic area. There was no cutting toward the legs as with Thompson, and she had minimal cutting to her breasts. This all happened along a roadside. I stared at what appeared to be her intestines, which were found strewn about ten feet from her body.

From all the pictures, I was unable to tell if either woman had a stab wound to the back, which seemed to be our killer's preferred first move. I wanted to know more, so I called Richard, hoping that he could point me to more information.

"Hello, dear boy! How are you?"

"Not bad, not bad at all. Actually, a bit perplexed . . ."

"Perplexed. How can I help you in that vein?"

"I was looking closer at the pictures from the Thompson and Dittmer murders overseas. Deeply disturbing, I might add. Are there any more pictures?"

"Unfortunately, that's all I have, and I am lucky to have those. For whatever reason, I hung on to them all these years after that conference in the late 1990s."

"Okay, do you have any international contacts to get more information?"

"The investigators working those cases have long since retired. The last that I heard, at least one of those investigations had been tied to a captured serial killer. I can't think of his name off the top of my head. I think that he was just doing what they do best and boasting about the number of murders he was responsible for when he confessed, and they lumped it on him to clear it. Neat and tidy to close the cases. But I think they're grossly mistaken. I don't think that he did it for reasons that would be better saved for another day's conversation."

"Do you happen to know if they were stabbed in the back like our victims? The pictures only show the frontal views on both women," I asked.

"That I cannot answer. Your murders were before, so he may have changed things. Don't be fooled by MO. Too many of you local investigators fall into that trap and try to line things up perfectly. These boys evolve as they work their way up the helix. You still have the helix, correct?"

"Of course."

"Oh good, good. You are quite the good little pupil."

"So, Richard, on the German case, why did the killer put her heart between her legs?"

"Aww, yes! Great question! Before I tell you my thoughts, what do *you* think?"

"Well, I think it's some type of symbolism and somehow the heart which represents life is near her vagina, which the killer thought was possibly evil?"

"You're partially correct. What you are missing in all of this is that she was a prostitute. The killer was probably playing a sarcastic ruse on her life and dirty vagina."

"Wow!" I said.

"Yes, yes." He hooted.

"And the cut marks to the breasts?"

"Piquerism, piquerism. He was cutting to experiment and to also desecrate a sexual female body part. Remember, it's all about control and power as part of an elaborate fantasy."

❧

I thought about how both of our murders had an interesting connection to a tunnel. Angela was on a bike path and within two to three hundred yards of a tunnel. Melanie was murdered very close to a tunnel, and we believed that our killer painted graffiti-type art inside the tunnel. I searched the internet. *What is the symbolism with the tunnels and death?*

I ran across an image that grabbed my attention. The cover of Ayn Rand's best-selling book, *Atlas Shrugged*, depicted a tunnel in the woods. I reached for my stack of the Thompson photos and the tunnel. I held the Thompson photo up to the screen noting it was remarkably similar. *Wow, that's eerie.*

I read up on *Atlas Shrugged*. The protagonist, John Galt, was a pilot. I remembered that our earlier research had uncovered that the US Air Force used a Cessna T-37B as a trainer plane, and it was nicknamed "Tweety

Bird." *Possible connection to our "Tweety" pilot theory (from the tunnel walls on Melanie's murder) and military / Air Force Base connection?* I looked intently at Ayn Rand and her connections to a tunnel. *What if our killer was a fan,* I thought?

From everything that I read about Rand, she was a staunch believer in people seeking out their own happiness and of people being rational and almost cherishing selfishness. *What if our killer clung to a belief that he could be happy disassembling women?* I wrote on my notepad: "Ayn Rand, *Atlas Shrugged*—centennial edition cover, John Galt—pilot, tunnel and mountain, train, perfect man, objectivism, fascinated with a guy named William Hickman, who murdered a twelve-year-old girl." *We are the living book.*

While I was researching Rand, I looked at tunnels, mountains, and death and stumbled upon the artist Salvador Dalí. I looked at his work with fascination. He was a surrealist, and everything he placed in his paintings had a meaning. I grabbed my notepad and next to "Rand" I wrote: "Salvador Dalí—blondes, religion, tunnels, mountains, train station, lots of detached body parts to include head and hands, deep symbolism, the Bleeding-Heart painting—which portrayed a woman cut open, who in turn looks kind of like the German victim."

My head ached from all of this, but I kept digging. The tunnel connection led me to Alfred Hitchcock. I grabbed my notepad again, and next to "Rand" and "Dalí" wrote: "Alfred Hitchcock—*Psycho* film—based in Phoenix, the likable criminal / the charming sociopath, trains *North by Northwest* film, transference of guilt, sexuality, blondes, tunnels with mountain, train, the perfect murder."

I drew a hard line across the page. I wrote: "pilot, mountains, tunnels, bunkers, Tweety—first training plane of Air Force, military killer with possible medical training and religion, likes water, well read, intelligent, Vietnam?"

I needed to discuss this with Richard.

"Richard, based on my research, Ayn Rand, Salvador Dalí, and Alfred Hitchcock all seemed to be involved with the themes of tunnels, blondes, and religious symbolism. It's way out there, but do you think our killer could have any fascination with the likes of these famous folks?"

"It's entirely possible. We're talking about an AE who is typically quite intelligent. Ergo, it would not surprise me that he was well read and may incorporate symbolism of this type into his own fantasies, murders."

"Good, I thought I was looking too much into this."

"No, these are some very interesting connections."

Could our local canal murders really be a part of an international wanton killing spree spanning decades?

CHAPTER 13
THE VIETNAM VET AND THE EYES

The entry on my screen had my full attention. I sat upright and peered at every word inscribed in the 1994 log. The entry read: "20 years ago, disemboweled two women and masturbated in guts. Recently released from Oregon penitentiary. Committed crime with surgeon's precision, using Gerber knife." *Disemboweled? Surgeon's precision? A surgeon would know how to quickly kill just like our killer. Double bonus if he was in the military.*

I twirled my pen and continued to read original investigator's notes which read, "P.O. [probation officer] said Samples was working on Monday, 11-9-92, and had not been out of town that he knows of." *That he knows of? Pretty weak to not explore further. I hope they did.*

I read an archived news article from 1981. Duane Samples was a psychology major at Stanford, an amateur boxer, and an avid skier. He served in the Vietnam War as a forward artillery officer and returned in 1967. *Okay, I'm interested. There's the military badass.* In 1975, he worked in Oregon as a drug counselor and befriended two women. He stopped by their house one night and savagely attacked them both with a ten-inch knife. One of the women somehow survived, and Samples was sentenced to life in prison. He used PTSD from Vietnam to get the governor to reduce his sentence to twenty years. The citizens of Salem and District Attorney Chris Van Dyke put up a fight to keep him in prison. Much to their dismay, he was out by the early 1990s.[1] I pulled out my scratch pad and wrote, "Vietnam vet, amateur boxer, mutilated two women, talk to DA Chris Van Dyke from Marion County, Oregon."

I left Chris a voicemail and spoke to him a few days later on the phone. As we were talking, I found out that Chris was the son of actor Dick Van Dyke. JJ, a millennial, was the only one on the squad who could not appreciate the connection to the great actor. Chris gave me a lot of interesting information. I discovered that when the original investigators served a search warrant on Samples's house after the murder, they found a living room painting depicting a man with a knife against a woman's throat. The kitchen had a painting with a horseman holding a stick with a human head attached. Samples had very violent art depicting Satanism and bizarre acts of violence in his bedroom. Also, he had a truss with knotted nylon ropes and notebooks with rambling words. They found his diaries, which contained numerous fantasies of eviscerating women, and evidence that he had stalked one of his victims. Samples had some bizarre infatuation with women killing him like a Christian martyr. *Wow, this guy looks good. Surgeon's precision, military, Christianity. We needed his DNA and now.*

After I spoke to Chris, adrenaline coursed through my body. I was excited again. I called Kelley and told her about Samples and my conversation with a great DA, who was Dick Van Dyke's son. With her normal steel trap of a memory, Kelley recalled the famous actor. She told me she would look into whether DNA was on file for Samples.

❧

I got pulled into meetings and boring supervisory tasks over the next few weeks, but I couldn't stop thinking about Samples. *A killer with a surgeon's precision and Vietnam vet! Located out of state, which explains why our killer stopped after Melanie in 1993! Could it be?*

Kelley called. *Here we go! Richard's guidance that 'He's in our files' is spot on!* Suddenly, a wave of frustration slapped me in the face. Samples was already in the national DNA system. He would have already been matched to our killer's DNA sample if it was him.

"Are you sure?" I asked.

"Yes, he's ruled out," Kelley said. She could feel my disappointment through the phone wire. "Sorry. Keep going."

"You're right. We might be in our late eighties when we find him, but we will," I said.

❧

Dom ran into my office, almost out of breath, and yelled, "My peeps found Thomas Worswick. They will bring him in."

"Great news. When?"

"Now. I'm gonna work my magic and get a confession."

"Okay, Dom. Is JJ with you?"

"Yes, he will monitor the interview."

The tip from the files read: "On 11-1-94 during canal stakeout, Officer Spitler observed van parked back in secluded area at 2225 West Mountain View. Seen two nights in a row. Both nights he had on no shirt, shorts only."

Worswick had a sexual assault attempt around the time of Angela's murder, where he attacked a blonde washing her car at the car wash close to Angela's apartment complex. He was stopped in the attack by a man who jumped in to help.

Later that evening, Dom called and said, "It's him, definitely him."

"What? Worswick? Did he confess?" My heart thundered.

"No, he didn't confess," Dom said in a dramatic manner, "but it's him. I saw it in his eyes. His eyes spoke to me!"

I regained my composure. "What did he say?"

"He denied everything but was super nervous. You know how you can look into a person's eyes and usually it looks normal?"

"Yeah," I said.

"I'm telling you, *it's him*. His eyes were dark, and his soul is dark."

"Well, I hope you're right, Dom. The ups and downs of this investigation are beginning to take a toll. The boxer in the ring can only sustain so many head shots."

"Don't worry this time—the Dominator's got it. Book me a spot on *Dateline*."

I rolled my eyes. "All I'm saying is just don't get too excited. We've been here before."

"I get it. It's him, though."

I had given Worswick's file to Dom a few weeks before. Despite a constant swell of joke-loving people around his cubicle and war stories galore, I had to admit Dom was efficient. Since our trip to Philadelphia, where Richard and his Vidocq experts told us the killer was in our files, Clark and I researched the files with a renewed energy. Clark moved from *A* forward. I started from *Z* and moved backward. We planned to meet in the middle at the *M* area. We isolated the ones we thought needed follow-up and gave them to the team. Dom, JJ, Marianne, and William, depending on workload, would track down and obtain the targeted lead's DNA.

֎

Marianne swooped into my office and said, "Boss, Dom has told everyone Worswick is the canal killer. And I mean everyone in the building and probably the entire police force."

"You didn't preface, but I understood you this time because you said Worswick. I'm excited, too, but I tried to tell Dom we've been down this road before. I want him to manage his expectations. The professor was your big disappointment, eh?"

"Yeah, Professor Brooks surprised me, but I'm over it now. The Lord will guide us. You heard anything back from Kelley on Worswick?" Marianne asked.

"Not yet. It usually takes a painful couple of weeks. They have their hands full over there with new cases. I don't want to bug her. If she calls, I will definitely ask her."

❧

Dom and JJ slid into my office.

"How's the S&P 500 look today?" Dom asked.

"It's up, I think," I said.

"Kid, you may want to push more into the stock market. Maybe stop buying so many Under Armour clothes for you and your fam," said Dom.

JJ rolled his eyes. "You need something, Sarge?"

"I've got another one for you guys from the files. Can you work with Kelley on it?"

"But Dom's all in on Worswick," said JJ.

Dom jumped in and said, "Yup, that's right. I told you, but I will tell you again. His eyes gave it away. It's him, but it's taking forever. Don't you have any pull over there, Hillman? I can't sleep at night. My wife is gonna leave me because I yell 'Worswick' like a hundred times a night."

"No, Kelley's crew works on a ton of cases. We're lucky they fit us in. Speaking of eyes, though, here's another one with an eye problem," I said. I slid the file on Scott Waitman over to them and gave them the details. The tip came shortly after Angela's murder in 1992. The caller said he had "wild, crazy eyes." Waitman was a maintenance worker who worked along the freeway and did irrigation and landscaping. He had served in the military and had a tattoo that read "Death Before Dishonor" above a sword on his left arm. He also had a lion on the inside of his right forearm and a US Army eagle on his left forearm. He had a dragon and skull on his right arm. Waitman's background was riddled with violence and property crimes. One of his exes described him as explosively angry.

Waitman was listed in an assault report against his ex-wife in 1993. He said to her, "Stop your fucking crying. No one will hear you in this neighborhood, and if the police come, you will be dead before they get through the front door. I've got a gun, and when you married me, it was 'til death do us part." He grabbed a buck knife, held it to her throat, and said, "I'll kill you, bitch, before you get out the door." His mother lived within five minutes of where Angela and Melanie were killed. Waitman was the victim of a homicide in 1997.

"Waitman sounds good, too. But I'm still betting the farm on Worswick," Dom said.

JJ took the file and said, "We'll handle it."

❧

For the next few weeks, every time I passed by Dom's cubicle he whispered, "Worswick. Heard anything?"

I whispered back, "No, you'll be the first to know, Dominator."

We all waited patiently. We were like kindergartners who obsessively waited for Santa Claus in November. Then, the phone call finally came and my heart rate shot up. This would be massive for the team, Dom, and the women's families.

Kelley's words hit like a torpedo in the hull of a submarine: "It's not Worswick."

I took in a deep breath and balled up a scratch piece of paper. I thanked her for her efforts and found Dom near the men's restroom. He was encircled by a group of detectives who clung to every word and waited for the punch line.

"Dom, can you come see me in my office after you're done?" I said.

"Sure, boss. Am I in trouble?"

"No, just have some news."

He yelled, "Worswick?! Should I get fitted for my Armani suit for the awards banquet?"

I walked away quickly. I didn't want to deliver the crushing news in front of the masses and hurt his ego. Dom was on my heels with bloodhound spirit.

"And?" Dom asked.

"It's not him. He's not our killer. I'm sorry. I know how much you liked him for it."

Dom looked like I punched him square in the stomach and knocked every ounce of oxygen out of him. His six-four frame collapsed into a seat. The court jester was speechless. No jokes. No words. He just sat there.

With a serious look I had never seen on the man, Dom said, "Can I have the rest of the day off, boss? I just need to clear my head. My instincts are normally spot on."

"Yes, of course, Dom, and take tomorrow if you need to. Just remember you're still a damn good detective. There are too many creepy guys out there. We just have to keep plodding through them. We have to keep looking. Take some time. Maybe the other guy with the eyes, Waitman, will be our killer, eh?"

He walked out, gathered his belongings, and swiftly headed for the exit. The detective who brought sunshine to a dark workplace was gone. I knew he would be devastated by the news. I just didn't know how devastated.

❦

JJ sat at his cubicle on the telephone. I figured he was on with a prosecutor based on his answers and knowledge that he was in the middle of multiple cases headed to trial. JJ made arrest after arrest, and the trials stacked up quickly. He hung up and shook his head.

"There's only one of me, but they want ten," JJ said.

"Can I get you some more help?" I asked.

"I'm good. I may complain, but you know I like being slammed."

"Yes, Mr. Efficient. So, you stopped by to see me earlier. Did you need something?"

"I have some more bad news on the canal murders."

"Ugh! We can't handle any more heartache. Dom is still mourning Worswick. This is becoming like a bad country song," I said. "Lay it on me."

"The other guy with the crazy eyes, Waitman."

"He's ruled out, too?" I asked. I grabbed his cubicle wall for support. Wave after wave of disappointment.

"Yeah, I ran into Kelley at a lab meeting this morning. She gave me the bad news and asked me if I could tell you. She said you were going to nickname her the Lead Killer if she kept delivering us bad news."

I shook my head in disgust. "Man, we can't catch a break. They say work the damn files, but the files are massive and chock-full of creepy guys. Oh, well. I'll get over it. Thanks for working that, guy."

I walked back to my office and sank into my chair. I rocked and stared out the window. My eyes locked onto the dry erase board and the words I had written after Dom's Worswick news: "Never Give Up!" *We must keep going.*

CHAPTER 14
THE GRIM SLEEPER AND THE PILOT

W illiam slid me an article. I adjusted my tired eyes from my paperwork and read the title "New Technique of Using Family's DNA Led Police to 'Grim Sleeper' Suspect: Los Angeles Police Chief Says New Technique Will 'Change Policing in America.'"[1]

Change policing in America?

I shut the door and hoped to send a clear signal of "I'm not here." The article was fascinating. It stated that the "Grim Sleeper" was responsible for killing at least ten young Black women and a man in Los Angeles from 1985 to 1988 and then again in 2007. LAPD had his DNA, like we did on the canal killer, but it never hit in the CODIS law-enforcement DNA database. According to the article, LAPD poured a mammoth number of hours and resources into solving the crimes but came up empty-handed until they tried a technique called familial DNA searching. In 2008, California instituted the familial DNA program to combat violent crime when there is "serious risk to public safety." It was the first state in the country to do so. When the killer's son's DNA was entered into the FBI-run database, LAPD investigators were alerted to a partial match. They followed this lead to the father, Lonnie David Franklin Jr., and confirmed his DNA matched that of the killer in the cases. The author suggested it was a huge win for LAPD and California, not to mention the victims' families and loved ones. It was an exciting new technique for the good guys to pursue justice.

My zeal was quickly tempered with the remainder of the article. It went on to describe the controversy surrounding this new technique. It read, "Familial DNA database searches have come under fire from privacy and civil liberty advocates."

I pulled up the FBI website and read the description of familial searching. Only four states, at the time, performed this type of testing: California, Colorado, Texas, and Virginia.

I picked up the phone and called Kelley. "Do you know anything about familial DNA testing?"

Without a tiny sliver of hesitation, she blurted, "Yes, I know all about it. LAPD caught that Grim Sleeper serial killer with it. It's what you need for the canal murders. That's why you're calling, right?"

"Wow! Yep, that's right."

"I remember talking to my boss about it recently. She said that the DPS lab was supposed to have it online this spring. However, it hasn't moved forward for reasons we don't know. Let me talk to her, and I'll call you back."

"Sounds good. No huge rush, though. Just looking at everything," I responded.

෴

She called back.

"Good news?" I asked with excitement. We desperately needed a break. We had just passed the three-year mark of our investigation.

Kelley replied, "Well, my boss said she ran into the director over there a few months ago, and he said that all the money that was earmarked for familial went to another project, rapid DNA. You remember me mentioning rapid DNA, right?"

"Yeah, that's the DNA that can be developed and compared in a matter of hours. Neat stuff, but it sure as hell doesn't help us much."

"Agreed," Kelley said.

"So, how can we try to get DPS to start doing it? Who do we need to talk to to light a fire, so to speak?"

"Well, we think that the chief's office needs to call over there," she said.

"Okay, I'll run it up the chain and see what I can do. Perfect fit for the canal murders, eh?"

"Yeah, it's perfect. Good luck."

I briefed my lieutenant on the new technique and slid him the article. He said he was buried in paperwork from a recent officer-involved shooting, but he would read it in the next few days and brief the commander. Later that week, the lieutenant said the article was great; he had spoken to the commander, and the commander agreed to speak with the chief about it. *Standby to standby*, I mused as my get-it-done background didn't always correlate to the speed, or lack thereof, of government work.

❧

After a few weeks of standing by, I finally got up the courage to ask the lieutenant if he had heard anything.

"No, sorry," he said, adding that he would follow up with the commander on it sooner rather than later.

The next day the lieutenant poked his head into my office and said, "So, Troy, I guess the chief did call over to the DPS crime lab and spoke to their director. It appears they diverted the funds to the rapid DNA project. They don't have the funding to proceed with the familial DNA project, currently. From what was said, they need some type of doctorate-level statistician to assist with these types of searches, and that's not in the budget right now. So, unfortunately, we're just plain out of luck on that strategy."

"Well, it was worth a try, and thanks for trying to make it work. Please express my thanks to the commander and the chief for inquiring about it."

"No problem. Good job in thinking outside the box and trying to use technology to solve those murders, Troy."

"Thanks, LT!"

❧

When I told Karyn about the Grim Sleeper and how he was caught, she said, "That is phenomenal. Now, wait, why can't you guys do that?"

"Because government moves like a sloth," I said.

❧

JJ and I went out for lunch. While we gobbled down sub sandwiches, JJ said Clark had given him a new lead from the files to look into.

"It looks like two tips came in for this guy," JJ said. "The first one read 'Donald Golder is a coworker of caller's wife's ex-husband. He was around the night Brosso was murdered, and the next day, he had a piece of a blood-soaked blanket.' The second call stated, 'Sally Green was babysitting for Golder and said he returned two hours late one night. She saw a bloody blanket in his apartment and felt Golder was acting strange that night.' Oh, and based on my research it looks like he's a pilot too."

"Wait! A pilot with two entries in the files?" I asked. A pilot related to Luke Air Force Base always made sense to our group due to the military connection. The word "Tweety" in the tunnel at Melanie's murder had possible connections to Air Force training planes used in the past. Pilots were definitely fair game in this investigation.

"Methinks it's a double whammy," said JJ with a smirk. He definitely respected Richard's brilliance and position in the profiler world, but JJ was amused by Richard's eccentric behavior and statements. Richard was one of a kind.

"Methinks is right. Ergo, Richard would love it."

JJ and I researched Golder, who lived in North Scottsdale. He appeared to be wealthy and was an independent businessman who liked to bike along the trails and canals. He was kind of a loner, divorced, two grown kids. His rap sheet was light. He flew planes and took lots of pictures in them.

"The guy is like a ghost," said JJ.

"Normally, your efficient nature would have his DNA to Kelley already," I said.

"I know. He seems to bounce around. Can we figure out a ruse to get his DNA?"

"I know some detectives in financial crimes. Let me see if I can set it up."

JJ and I met with the detectives and briefed them on Golder. They agreed to set up a ruse and get him to lick an envelope. We sat back and waited. We had become good at that.

❧

A few weeks passed, and I got the call that the financial crimes detectives met Golder and obtained his DNA. JJ got the DNA and handed it off to Kelley, and the waiting game started again.

"You think it's him?" asked JJ.

"I've been wrong many times, but he's flown under the radar—no pun intended. He appeared twice on the list. That's gotta count for something, right?"

"Usually, they have something on their rap sheet, though. Didn't Richard say they started fires as juveniles, engaged in Peeping Tom activities, or stole women's panties?"

"Yes, he did. But maybe Golder did those things and is too slick to get caught? Slick enough to kill two young women along a canal and go undetected for over two decades, eh?"

"Maybe," said JJ.

"We'll know soon." I wanted to call Kelley and ask, but I knew the drill. I just needed to be patient. The agony of waiting!

❧

The call came in from Kelley. Rejection had become our first name. Yet, I still had a positive attitude.

I blurted out, "You know one of these days we're gonna be right."

"Yes, you will. I have faith in you and your team—just not today. Golder is out."

I sighed and shook my head. "Okay, we'll keep going."

"Keep sending them over."

After giving JJ the bad news, I went home and told Karyn all about it. She supported me and allowed me to wallow in my frustrations. Then she said, "You will solve this thing, Troy. I just know it."

❧

I stared at my dry erase board. Familial DNA could not help us, and the names that at one time held pure excitement were systemically struck down. I had written the phrases "pathology trumps intellect" and "sarcastic ruses" on the board when I returned from the trip to the Vidocq Society. At first, I struggled to see what Richard meant in terms of pathology trumping intellect. I didn't want to admit it to him. He was a well-read and brilliant man, so I needed to figure it out on my own and apply it to our investigations.

Finally, something clicked. I saw that pathology trumps intellect in the world around me. High-ranking generals and sports figures lost their careers, their families, and everything else after they were unfaithful and caught. Their intellect told them not to do it because it was way too risky, but their pathology trumped their intellect, and they acted on it. I also saw it when I watched football games. A player right in front of an official would deliver a late hit to another player. A flag would inevitably be thrown, and the team would be heavily penalized. The collective roars: "Why would he do that? Is he stupid?" I wanted to yell, "No, it's his pathology. His anger trumped his smarts. He knew better." When I finally figured it out, I admitted it to my mentor, Richard.

"Dear boy, you're right. The news is riddled with it! Scandals abound. Yes, yes, yes! Pathology trumps intellect every time. It's the reason serial killers eventually get caught. They may be quite good at their craft, but they eventually screw it up. Their pathology kicks in, they lose control, and then they leave something important behind or get caught where they shouldn't be. Bundy, Dahmer, BTK, they all did it."

"Fascinating."

"Now that I am giving you a lesson, please tell me the sarcastic ruses in your murders," Richard said.

I told him about the piece of plywood at a secondary scene for Angela that read "I cut that bitches head off." I told him about the tunnel pictures with Tweety from Melanie's murders.

"They think the cops are stupid. They love to mock you guys. I wouldn't doubt it if your killer showed up at the press conferences after the murders. They do it quite often."

"Quite risky."

"Yes, it is. But they get to relive the thrill of their murder. They get a rush from it. Remember, the murder is not over until the killer is done."

"Huh?"

Richard explained how the AE subtypes would keep trophies, pictures, videotapes, and so on to relive their fantasies and keep the murders and associated victims alive in their minds. They would frequently masturbate to these objects.

"They don't cover this in homicide 101 training, Richard," I said.

"No, dear boy. This is advanced stuff. That's why you have me."

༄

Since our baby's birth in July, I took turns with Karyn sleeping in the nursery. During those many nights while our baby fed from the bottle, my mind annoyingly toggled to the haunting words of my close friend Mike, who had told me over the previous three years, "This is *your* case." Mike was there the day I met Karyn, was the best man in my wedding, and knew me like a baseball catcher knows his glove. Keenly, he knew that the canal murders were eating at me beneath my joy for the gifts bestowed upon me in my personal life, like Karyn and our baby. *This is* your *case* echoed in my mind while I held the bottle in the dark. In fact, when he first said those words to me on a trip to the boxing gym years prior, I said, "What do you mean?"

"Mr. Hillman," Mike said, "every good detective has one or two big cases that eat at them. That's not to say that they don't care about the others. It's just the one or two that weigh on, and frankly, haunt him the rest of his career and into retirement if not solved."

My finance sleuth buddy couldn't be more right, and I begrudgingly knew it. In fact, my whole team, like Russ Davis, the original detective, and a host of others who spent countless hours trying to spot the creepy maggot, would indeed take these two women's cases with them into retirement and onto their death beds. *It's been three years, and we're no further than the day we started. My, my, this is* your *case*, I thought, dismayed. I embraced sleep before the next volley of piercing cries erupted.

CHAPTER 15
THE FATHER AND THE DECEASED

JJ ran into my office. "We just got a call from a woman in Colorado. She said that she thinks her father is the canal killer."

"That's bizarre. Out of the blue, she just calls and throws that out? Her father?"

"I guess he just passed away, and she decided to come forward with information."

Dom jumped in. "She said that her father told her that he had done some really bad things to some young women in Phoenix. She asked him if it was the two women near the canals, and he got angry and threatened her."

"Okay."

JJ continued. "He used to beat her, her sister, and her mother. Everyone in the house was deathly afraid of him. She saw him a couple of times with a hunting-style knife, and he was apparently very protective of it."

"What's his rap sheet look like?" I asked.

"The usual stuff from a drunk, angry man," JJ said. "DUIs, assaults at bars, domestic violence."

"Any sexual assaults, molestations, or the like?"

"No, not that he's been done for," retorted JJ.

"Military?"

"He was in the Marine Corps," Dom added.

JJ said, "I talked to Kelley, and she said they could construct his DNA enough to rule him out if they had the daughter's DNA."

CHASING DOWN THE ZOMBIE HUNTER

The next week Dom and JJ flew to Colorado and met with Wilbur Schultz's daughter and obtained her DNA for comparison. The DNA was handed off to Kelley and her team. The agonizing waiting game began yet again.

"Did you get any more information from Schultz's daughter?" I asked.

"Nope, she was adamant that he said he did 'bad' things," said Dom.

"Do you think it's him?" I asked. "And Dom, don't bring up Worswick and how you think it still might be him." The squad had ribbed Dom about Worswick. We needed the lighthearted jokes to keep us on point.

"I'm never gonna live that down. It was in his eyes," Dom said.

JJ said, "Who knows, at this point, if it's the killer. It very well could be. We wouldn't have to put the families through a painful trial at least. Wilbur being dead and all."

"I agree with the Kid," said Dom. "Who knows? You could be the killer for all we know, boss," said Dom.

JJ smirked and said, "I would put more odds on Clark." JJ had a deep respect for Clark, but he liked to torment him.

"He's not even here to defend himself," I said.

"I'm sure he's somewhere cussing about the trash put in his cubicle by the potluck people," said JJ.

"Back to our murders. We don't know. Maybe?" I asked.

"Could be Wilbur. Could not be Wilbur. We just wait, like always," Dom said.

Over the next few weeks, when I walked about the office, they would ask, "Kelley? Anything? Schulz? Just stop asking?" I would just shake my head and keep going.

The call eventually came from Kelley. Wilbur Schulz was not our killer. Dom asked to leave work early again. JJ just shook his head and joked, "Our team is like the Illinois football team. A continual losing effort." He took a stab at my college alma mater, but I enjoyed his humor at this point. He was right on both accounts. Illinois had been mediocre for years in football, and we were spinning our wheels on the canal murders, lead after lead. *What if Richard was wrong and the killer was NOT in our files?* Up to this point, I had successfully, and possibly naïvely, shut out all doubts. Now, my mind was saturated with them. All we could do was just keep meticulously going through those files.

I walked into the Marriott near Phoenix's Sky Harbor Airport early. My team was overwhelmed with a massive number of court cases and forensic hits. We also battled a mind-numbing and growing list of cold cases, over 2,750 at this point, each requiring follow-up and time. And remember, we were covering only cold cases in the city of Phoenix! That was time we didn't have, time tugged away from justice for Angela and Melanie. *Maybe the Vidocq Society scholars will give us a boost,* I thought. We all looked forward to seeing Richard and his entourage.

Dom and JJ prepared the welcome table. Despite doing their regular grueling investigator duties, those two were remarkable. They arranged all the moving variables for the weeklong training. The list of attendees was large and included investigators from not only Arizona, but also California, Nevada, Texas, and New Mexico. The word had spread that this high-level training was unlike any other they had ever attended during their law enforcement careers. Despite the increased use of DNA, the number of cold cases in the country had grown remarkably. Profilers like Richard could be of great assistance to the average detective. The guidance of "he's in your files," "pathology trumps intellect," and "sarcastic ruses" would prove fundamental to our investigation and many others in the years ahead. But I was getting antsy for it to pay off now.

Richard was in his unique form while he taught the helix and subtypes portion of the training. I don't think the audience knew what to do with him. He was unlike any instructor that they had ever been around. One minute in the room with him and everyone could tell that he was beyond brilliant and spoke in a very polished, almost aristocratic manner. At points, he would devolve into raw sarcasm and could ridicule harshly, but with clean language. I found him hilarious and intriguing. Only in private, and typically after a few strong cocktails, would this polished gentleman curse, and curse he did.

When Richard finished his block of instruction on his subtypes, he showed a homemade movie clip made by a young homosexual serial killer. He said, "You'll see some kiss and giggles"—he gestured air quotes with his hands—"and then the boy begins . . . I can't say where I got this movie from, but it's real folks, real!" The video showed, in graphic and horrifying detail, the deranged killer stabbing his roommate to the point of absolute overkill. Blood struck the camera and splattered the walls. The audience watched the killer cut off a huge chunk of the roommate's buttocks. Richard peered at the stunned group of supposed seasoned investigators with a smile and said, "You see, our boy here apparently cooked that chunk of buttocks for dinner because the police later found a small portion left in the skillet. There's a reason I wanted this block of instruction right before lunch." He cackled for minutes. I had seen a lot of gore and killing, but this live-action cutting was chilling. I felt squeamish watching it.

I saw Kelley before the afternoon session started and said, "Where's Karl?" Karl was an experienced DNA lead who had seen just about everything in his time.

"He didn't want to come back." She laughed. "He was too traumatized by Richard's video this morning."

"You're kidding?"

"No, it was just too much."

"I found it slightly disturbing."

"Me, too."

"I will have to mention that to Richard. I think he will find it humorous."

"I can see that."

❧

Later that afternoon, Richard got up for another block of instruction. He began with "Did everyone enjoy their lunch after this morning's lesson? Anyone use a skillet to fry up some delicious chunk of raw meat?" He laughed forcefully. I laughed, too, but most just shook their heads in disgust. "So, from kiss and giggles and AEs, we go to this instruction on autoeroticism. I think you will find it equally riveting," he said. He smiled from ear to ear. For the next couple of hours, we saw everything from crime scene photos of men dressed in women's attire hanging from ropes to homemade videos of men in women's underwear hanging from trees masturbating to passing cars. It was extremely deviant behavior, to say the least. Richard made the point that a lot of these look on the surface like suicides, but they were accidents. "Only the best of investigators would see this subtlety, and only those trained by yours truly," Richard stated emphatically with an underlying grin.

Part of what Richard and Vidocq offered during the training were breakout sessions where detectives could brief them on their cases. They would ask questions and give feedback, much like "solving cold cases over lunch" in Philadelphia. It was a phenomenal benefit to have expert opinions on individual cases.

Richard and Vidocq taught investigators what no other law enforcement training taught them, which was how to hunt the most advanced of monsters (i.e., serial killers) and how to look beyond what was in front of you, just like the autoerotic investigations. They truly wanted to help. In contrast, most trainers seemed to focus on more "typical" murders, which would have involved those close to the victim or those who would have known the victim. Thus, the methodology for solving the case would have been entirely different.

On the last evening, Dom, Clark, the Kid, and I met with Richard and his colleagues in a suite for drinks. We discussed the canal murders and all our futile efforts to date. While a few members said, "You might be right; he might be dead," I looked down with frustration. Richard nudged me and said, "Dear boy, do you remember what I told you when we first met in Philadelphia?"

I looked straight at him as I drank my beer and said, "Yes, I do—he's in your files."

"Yes, yes, yes! Indeed! You must keep looking!"

I grinned and appreciated his zeal, but I was also beginning to wonder if we would ever find our killer. *Maybe he was indeed deceased? Maybe we were fools for going on this journey?*

CHAPTER 16
THE THANK-MAS GATHERING

A local barbecue restaurant was a peculiar choice for a team-building event squarely centered between Thanksgiving and Christmas. My corny name for the between-holiday gathering was Thank-mas. The smell of glazed ribs and tender brisket greeted the nostrils before the door even opened. Smothered mash potatoes and biscuits were made from scratch and instantly dissolved in your mouth. The servers belted out inviting pleasantries upon entry. It was my kind of place. Small-town feel, just like home.

We needed to step away from the grind, even if it was just for a feel-good lunch. The emotional roller coaster of the canal murders hit us all differently. We were not robots, and these frustrations often manifested in subtle ways. Most of us exchanged jokes to escape the reality of what we had seen done to Angela and Melanie and compartmentalized it. Others might cuss a lot or tip the numbing bottle at home. I tried my best to keep an eye out and made efforts to ease up on their other duties—thousands of cold cases, courtroom testimony, outside agency assists, research, etc.

The good and bad of our personal lives didn't get put on hold, either. We all had children and aging parents. Karyn and I just welcomed a baby girl into the world. JJ, Kelley, and Mark all had preteens. Dom had young teenagers, while William and Clark had older ones. Marianne had an early start and had a grown son. With each of these elite team members, I sat proudly at the head of the table and knew that our children were at the top of the priority list. Family came first, and everyone needed time to make sure they focused on all that was good in their lives before we got back to work hunting down the bad.

To wit, I also set time aside for a few quirky team bonding times, and this afternoon, several weeks after the Vidocq conference, was one of those.

"Look at Marianne's getup," said Dom. Marianne had a festive red sweater and green pants on.

"And where's your Christmas spirit, Dom?" I asked.

"Back East, where it's cold and where I'm from," Dom said.

"You would look good in an elf costume, Dom," said William.

JJ jumped in and said, "Methinks he's more of a bad Santa."

"OK, clowns, let's do this before our meal," I said. "Let's play a game I played at the end of my academy days. It's called 'Who Am I?'"

The group shot me a do-we-have-to look. They knew it was a team-building exercise.

"Look, I know it's goofy, but we've all been grinding away at the canal murders for more than three years. Ergo, we need some fun time away." I winked. "I'm sure dear boy Richard would love this exercise."

"Methinks fun is more like Vegas, boss," said William.

"You're right, but this is the best I've got. I've put together a list with descriptors. Your job is to write a team member name next to it." I handed out the papers and pencils.

The List:
- I am the son of a pastor.
- My father was a successful land developer in southern Arizona.
- I coach my son's football team.
- I just bought property up in Flagstaff for my son to attend Northern Arizona University.
- My wife is a police officer, and she works in community events.

- My wife is a former grant writer and wants to be a teacher.
- I am studying to be a forensic nurse so I can help people once I retire.
- I wear Under Armour clothing all the time.
- I love attending and watching professional sports.
- I get up at 3 A.M. to feed my horses and care for them.
- My wife is a burglary detective.
- My son loves to compete in bike races, and my daughter wants to be a surgeon.
- I am a former stockbroker.
- I am from Alaska.
- I had a bulldog named Morty.

After about ten minutes, I said, "Okay, team, let's score them. Let's read them out loud." I read each one line by line, and the appropriate answer. I knew each of them pretty well.

I am the son of a pastor—JJ

"You never told me that, Kid," said Dom.

"You never asked. You're too busy talking!" snapped JJ.

My father was a successful land developer in southern Arizona—Marianne

"What? No comments, Dom or Kid?"

"Southern royalty," said JJ.

I coach my son's football team—Clark

"Clark, you go easy on the poor boys, right?" asked Marianne.

"Of course. They do a lot of running when they don't listen," Clark said.

I just bought property up in Flagstaff for my son to attend Northern Arizona University—William

My wife is a police officer, and she works in community events—Dom

"What does she see in you, Dom?" asked Mark.

"I've been trying to figure that out. Way above my pay grade," said Dom.

My wife is a former grant writer and wants to be a teacher—Mark

I am studying to be a forensic nurse so I can help people once I retire—Marianne

"Always showing off and helping people," said JJ.

"Kid!" Marianne snapped.

I wear Under Armour clothing all the time—JJ

"What? It's comfortable," said JJ.

"Comfortably expensive," jabbed Dom.

I love attending and watching professional sports—Clark

"Clark, don't you barricade yourself inside of a room all day on fantasy football Sundays?" I asked.

"Maybe. It's serious stuff," Clark said.

I get up at 3 A.M. to feed my horses and care for them—Marianne

"That's early, girlfriend," said Dom.

My wife is a burglary detective—William

"She works harder than I do," said William.

My son loves to compete in bike races, and my daughter wants to be a surgeon—Mark

"Mark, your kids are so smart and well behaved. You've done a nice job," said Marianne.

"It's all my wife," said Mark.

I am a former stockbroker—Clark

I am from Alaska—Kelley

"How did you end up in this burning inferno called Phoenix?" asked Dom.

"I didn't have a choice. I came here as a child," Kelley said.

I had a bulldog named Morty—Kelley

"Love the bulldog breed! Drumroll. Looks like we have a winner for the massage," I said.

Dom said, "Hey yo, I dominated!"

"Not so fast," I said. "It's William. William, you get the massage."

"It was rigged!" said JJ.

William told the table about his PhD. Many of us had heard it many times before, but we always found it amusing.

The entrées were finally served. Before we dug in, I made the team go around the table and tell what they were thankful for. A consistent theme emerged. They were all thankful for family and their work family.

We feasted on the delicious barbecue and fixings, and the chatter was limited. After lunch, I heard them tease each other about some new personal facts they learned in the exercise.

Before we left, Marianne told the group how proud she was of them. "I know we're supposed to just enjoy and leave work at work, but I have faith in this group. We will solve the canal murders and give those girls and their families justice." Her positivity continued to radiate.

I later heard rumors that the team actually enjoyed the "goofy" event despite some of the good-natured ribbing I took going into it. *Let the blessings continue.*

CHAPTER 17
THE DNA DOCTOR

I listened to the voicemail message.

"Boss, this is Marianne. I got a strange voice mail from some lady who says she's a . . . a . . . a forensic genealogist, whatever that is? She wants to meet with us. I wasn't sure what to do with this, so I forwarded her message to you . . . So, well, here you go."

Forensic what? I thought. *Did she say genealogist? Like Ancestry.com genealogy? What is this all about?* I listened and a woman's voice spoke clearly and professionally identifying herself as Dr. Colleen Fitzpatrick from a company named Identifinders. She said, "Hello, yes, Detective Ramirez, I understand that you work in cold case homicide. I am sorry for the short notice, but I am going to be in Phoenix in late October at a DNA conference and wondered if I could meet with you and your fellow detectives." Dr. Fitzpatrick continued with her contact information and a polite request for a return phone call.

I called her. She told me she was a forensic genealogist and did unique work with DNA to come up with family surnames. She had helped the military, historical societies, and law enforcement in the past. She told me she would be lecturing at a DNA conference in Phoenix in a few days and wanted to meet with my team if we had time.

"Interesting," I said. "So, let me get this straight. You can look at DNA and give us a name?"

"Yes, Troy, I can. Well, not always, but many times. It's too complex to explain over the phone, which is the reason for wanting to meet in person."

"Fascinating, but as you are probably aware, we creatures here in law enforcement are absolute skeptics of most things outside of our core training and current practices. So, let's do this—please send me all your information—including your education and experience, and we'll discuss and go from there. That work?"

"Great! Thank you, Troy. I hope to hear from you soon."

I was excited but skeptical. This was scientific stuff and multiple rungs above my pay grade. If there's one thing I learned over the years as a sergeant, when in doubt, use your resources to find experts and consult with them. I decided to call my shrewd DNA friend over at the lab. Kelley read forensic journals for fun. If anyone I could trust would know, it was Kelley.

I started, "So, I received an interesting call this morning from a woman claiming to be a . . . a . . . a . . ." I checked my notes. "Forensic genealogist. Have you ever heard of this? A DNA doctor? Is it weird science? Voodoo?" I said, half kidding but half serious. Kelley and I both knew that numerous people had called in over the years wanting to help us solve cold cases and especially assist on the heinous canal murders. Some of these "helpers" were genuine but misguided on what we could collaborate on, and others bordered on the fringes of madness. Both of us also realized psychics had peppered our files with theories, and for many in law enforcement, psychics were completely out of the question for consultation and utilization in a homicide investigation, essentially akin to witchcraft.

Kelley said, "No, not really. I do know that the DNA research world is exploding, and genealogists have been using Ancestry.com, 23andMe, and other sites for research."

"Okay, so I have a favor to ask. This forensic genealogist said that she was coming to Phoenix in a few days to attend some weeklong DNA conference. Could I arrange for you and your scientists to meet her?"

Kelley said, "Yeah, we're all going to that conference as well. I did see some block in the training about forensic genealogy, come to think of it."

"Interesting. So, Kelley, is there any way that I could arrange a blind-date style meeting before we sit down and talk with her? You could give me a barometer on her to rule out any psychic vibes and figure out what exactly she does, dumbing it down, of course, for this nonscientific accountant?"

"Not a problem. I think it will be interesting. What can it hurt?"

Colleen sent me an abundance of information on her company, Iden-tifinders, and her robust background. I pored through all of it and was impressed not only that she had a PhD from Duke University, but that she had also been heavily involved in a host of historical, government, military, and law enforcement projects and cases. From identifying children on the *Titanic* to soldiers on the battlefield from many moons ago, Colleen had given names to the nameless and much-needed closure to grieving families.

❧

A few days went by, and Kelley called me. She told me she spoke with the forensic genealogist the day before and thought she had a unique background and perspective on new techniques for DNA research. Kelley believed she was legitimate and could help us out on the canal murders. "It's worth a shot at this point," she added.

The following day the Kid and Dom picked Colleen up at a local resort and brought her downtown to headquarters. Colleen was rather short (at least compared to six-foot-four Dom) and appeared to be in her early to mid-fifties. She had a loose perm and a conservative short haircut, and wore a professional suit complete with scholarly eyeglasses. With the demeanor of an Ivy League college professor, Colleen spoke eloquently to our team for forty-five minutes, serving up an in-depth presentation on how she could take the numbers from a DNA profile on a male and predict ancestry, including geographical origination of male paternal relatives, and even give investigators a surname.

Colleen stepped out of the conference room to use the restroom, and I could see the scientific confusion going from DNA strands to names on each of the detectives' faces, yet I also saw fascination. The room evolved into a quiet and brooding library as the pupils digested the professor's lecture.

"Worth a shot on the canal murders, guys and gal?" I asked, breaking the silence from the normally chatty group. As I went around the conference table one by one, each indicated an emphatic yes. I could feel the excitement and embrace of this new forensic technique, not to mention a renewed hope. Then, I sighed and said, "Sounds great, but we have to somehow sell this new science to the upper chain of command and somehow get them to write a check for seven hundred and fifty dollars sooner rather than later."

Clark, in his serious tone, said, "The way I see it is that we've got to do something. He may be in our files, like Richard and his Vidocq people say, but it's gonna take *forever* to comb through that creepy canal list. Those leaders"—he rolled his eyes—"need to understand that we, the investigators, know what's best for these cases."

I laughed, as I knew Clark was right in that we, the investigators, had boots on the ground and knew best how to move our cases forward, but many of the leaders above us were afraid to take a chance out of fear of falling from their perceived upward trajectory to the top and landing in an undesirable position on graveyards somewhere. Sadly, police work has not historically been known as a place to try out new ideas and was rather punitive to those who messed up trying to innovate for the better. This was indeed a stark contrast to the business world, where ingenuity was rewarded, and failure was expected and completely accepted. Unfortunately for me and the team, cold cases called for ingenuity and cutting-edge techniques such as forensic genealogy. The room abandoned the brooding library vibe and broke out in abundant chatter until Colleen returned to the room.

Dom and JJ prepared to take her back to the resort. I told them to work on her to get a discounted or free price, especially since she would be helping on such high-profile cases as the canal murders. I thought the upper chain of command would go for it if it didn't cost us anything. We would have nothing to lose.

When the two returned, they stopped by my office. "No go," said the Kid, with a rare frown on his face. "She wouldn't budge on that price."

Dom smiled and added, "I tried everything—playing on her heartstrings, the huge publicity with a win on these cases, the awful things done to Angela and Melanie . . . everything—even bribery, a seat on the Supreme Court, a Hollywood movie deal, tickets to the Super Bowl, everything."

"It's okay guys. Thanks for your efforts. She deserves to get paid, but it's just so hard to convince the chain with a price tag attached. I am gonna speak to the lieutenant and push it up the chain. In the scheme of things, seven hundred and fifty dollars is a tiny crumb in the massive budget of the police department—and the city, for that matter. Not to mention that we spend over one thousand dollars every time we travel to get DNA on these cases. It's worth a shot to use this new technology, right?"

I stepped into my lieutenant's office. I told him about the voicemail from Colleen Fitzpatrick with a PhD from Duke and added that she's a forensic genealogist. I slid Colleen's bio sheet and work-up to him. I said, "She studied genealogy and family trees, and she's been able to help the military and other law enforcement agencies. This doctor can somehow look at a DNA sequence and give a surname. It's based on the Y-hits, which is the male line. So, every male in your male line will share a common Y-DNA marker. She can isolate it based on the DNA sequencing. I had Kelley meet her to discuss her process." I gave him a ton of information and could not control my excitement.

"She a doctor of witchcraft and weird science?"

I said, "I get it. It's totally groundbreaking and out of the box. Again, I totally get it, but for seven hundred and fifty dollars she will look at our unknown male DNA on the canal murders and hopefully give us a surname."

"Hopefully?" he said, studying my reaction.

"Yeah. She won't know for sure until she is able to look at the DNA sequencing and study what's out there on the genealogical websites. As you know, we've been grinding away on the canal murders for three-plus years now. Richard from Vidocq states emphatically that he's in our files. The problem is that there are just too many names in our files. They're all creepy maggots, and we don't have the resources to flush them all out. Clark and I will be in nursing homes before we get through that awful list from the files. If she could give us a surname for that price, then we would have something more focused to work with. To me, there's nothing to lose, as we're not sharing the secrets of our investigations with her. She will only get the unknown DNA sequence from our lab. It's worth a shot for seven hundred and fifty dollars, as investigative travel costs us over one thousand dollars a pop. Dom and JJ tried to get her down to on the house, as it would be a win-win, but she won't budge on her price."

"You're always pushing the envelope. However, that's what Cold Case must do, I figure. I agree with you, but the bosses will have lots of questions before we give this witch doctor the green light." He smiled. "Let's vet her with the military, the agencies she's claimed to have worked with, and the county attorney. If they're all good with her, then write it up in a memo."

JJ and I spoke to a host of law enforcement agencies, who gave Colleen glowing reviews, but the military unfortunately "refused comment." I desperately hoped this would not create an issue. I reached out to a seasoned prosecutor over at the county attorney's office. I told him this new technique might help us. He had been a newer attorney during the canal murders, and he wanted it solved before he retired. The prosecutor conferred carefully with his group, and they decided this new technique couldn't hurt the case and would be just a lead. We would need to get DNA regardless.

It took several months to get the chain of command to approve the seven-hundred-fifty-dollar expenditure. It was a tiny speck in a multimillion-dollar budget for a brand-new gamble on DNA technology. Once I had the green light, we provided Colleen with the DNA numbers she needed and waited for a miracle.

Even though Karyn and I exchanged yawns from the baby-feeding frenzies of late, she was absolutely fascinated with my recap of what Colleen said and the groundbreaking possibility of this cutting-edge technique. "Phoenix PD could be the first to use genealogy to catch a serial killer, eh?" she said.

"Yes, just maybe."

Colleen was all business and said, "Troy, I just sent you an email with my results. The surname that I came up with is Miller. From my research, it appears this family originated in England and came to America, settling in North Carolina. I cannot be one hundred percent sure, but it was a solid match."

I pulled out my notepad and jotted down "Miller."

"Wow!" I drew a long breath. "That's excellent news, Colleen!"

"Troy, good luck and let me know if you need anything else," and she hung up the phone.

Miller, eh? I thought. That's no Smith, but it is common. I toggled from negative to positive. I heard the words of eccentric crime scene assessor Richard Walter resonating: "He's in your files. No doubt about it."

Back to the files. But at least this time, the net was a bit smaller.

CHAPTER 18
THE DISCOVERY OF FILE 668

Mark popped his head in and handed me a worksheet. "You see, my organization is exemplary! I found five references to Millers in our files. File 155 pertains to a Brian Miller. File 430 lists a James Miller. File 668 references a Bryan Miller. And there's a file without a number that references a psychic named Karen Miller. Oh, and this wasn't on the list, but there was a Bill Miller who lived in Angela's complex in apartment 3132 during the time of the murder. He was on the roster provided by the apartment complex management. I grabbed the files from the basement."

I felt my heart thunder. This was it. This was the true test of *the* theory, one I had not heard of before our visit with Richard and his Vidocq Society colleagues. A theory on the serial killer that boldly commands there's more than a 90 percent chance he's in our files. The file would stem from one of the following scenarios: He was interviewed during the original investigation, he was documented around the crime scene, he called or wrote in to police to insert himself, he told someone something specific or someone saw him doing something bizarre and they called it in, or another law enforcement agency called him in. It was the theory we clung to for hope after our multiyear hunt. Yet, I would definitely take those odds in Vegas.

File 155 Brian Miller (Logged November 10, 1992)

An anonymous caller did not want to leave her name. She stated that she had met Miller through a *New Times* ad. He always follows her around and was very violent. There was a note: "Might want to look at him." Two reports were listed: one was from 1991 (threats), and the other was from 1992 (interfering with judicial procedures).

This one was marked "workable." The packet also had a full page of handwritten notes. The assigned investigator tracked down Brian Miller and asked him questions. Brian denied knowing anyone at Woodstone Apartments (Angela's complex). He admitted to riding a bike, but he claimed that he didn't know Angela and had never met her before. There was nothing else in the file, and it appeared the investigator was satisfied with this conversation.

I did a quick work-up in our system and noted that Brian Miller had been arrested for a felony in 2009. *With that information, his DNA should be in CODIS and would have been a hit with our unknown profile, right?* I made a note to verify this with Kelley.

File 430 James Miller (Logged March 23, 1994)

An officer had contacted three subjects (James Miller, Yolanda Hines, and William Rivera) in a van by the canal on March 22, 1994, around midnight. The subjects claimed that their van had broken down, and they pushed the van over by the canal. Rivera had been driving.

The investigator who worked the tip had closed it out, saying that the three individuals had been seen around the interstate and Dunlap, with the woman begging for money. He further indicated that they appeared to be passing through the area. James Miller had minimal criminal history.

It might be worth getting his DNA at some point, but nothing too exciting here, I thought.

Karen Miller (Logged November 15, 1992)

This woman rambled about coming up with a number 8 and a sign of the zodiac. She added that she wasn't in a cult but was into numerology. She added, "I think that he stalked her . . . I thought it was her boyfriend . . . Scorpio is part of the zodiac . . . I don't think her boyfriend did it but may have had something to do with it. The suspect smoked Camels."

The form was marked "unworkable" and closed out.

Okay, nothing exciting here. On to the next, I thought.

Bill Miller

Mark had highlighted Bill Miller's name on Angela's apartment complex roster. There was nothing else mentioned in the files. I did a quick work-up and there was really nothing on this guy. *It might be worth tracking him down and getting his DNA, but again nothing exciting here.*

Bryan Miller, File 668 (Logged May 26, 1994)

Now, just what do we have here? I thought as I grabbed the half-inch-thick file and cast my full attention toward the packet. An anonymous caller stated that Bryan had a female's bodysuit in his possession a few days before Melanie's murder. He worked at St. Vincent de Paul and was known to bring women's undergarments home from work.

I hurriedly turned to page two, thirsty for more knowledge.

Memorandum Typed Up by an Investigator,
Dated May 31, 1994, and Titled "Information"

The subject was Bryan Miller, white male, 21 years old, born in Hawaii, six-foot tall, skinny, and wears glasses. It was noted that he rides a racing type of bike and wears a helmet with the number 46 on it and "Miller" on top. It read:

On 5-26-94 at approximately 1630 hours, I answered the Homicide telephone and received a telephone call from an anonymous female caller. She related the following information about Bryan Miller:

About the time of the article in the newspaper about the bodysuit and the girl's murder at Metrocenter, Bryan was in possession of a bodysuit. Bryan's roommate, Randall [sic] McGlade, told her that about the time of the girls' murder, he saw a similar bodysuit in their room. Apparently, they were in the process of becoming roommates at the time. The last time Randall [sic] saw the body suit was either at the time of the murder or a few days before or after.

She said Bryan was apparently involved in a knife attack when he was a juvenile and spent time in prison for it. She thinks this was in the Phoenix area.

Bryan works for the St. Vincent de Paul warehouse, M–F 0700–1530. He often would bring home women's undergarments and clothing. As far as she knows, he has never had a girlfriend and has bad relationships with his mother and grandmother.

She does not know where he lives but thinks it may be around 20th Street or 7th Avenue and Camelback Road.

Bryan rides his bike to work in the morning, and he and

Randy go home together. They also go to the same church, and Randy told her Bryan circles names of church members who have young girls in their families. She thinks it's a Catholic church like St. Mary's or something similar.

On 5-31-94 she called me back to let me know Bryan was born in Hawaii.

(I got the impression when talking to this caller that she also works at St. Vincent de Paul and may have access to computer information. She may work in the office there.)

I noticed a handwritten scribble near the margins: "Roommate does not want [illegible]."

File 668 and this particular Miller grabbed my full and undivided attention. I abruptly cleared my schedule for the rest of the morning and kept the office door closed to the pestering outside world.

I turned the page of the packet and found what appeared to be a printout of a comprehensive search and listing of "McGivney" to "McGlasson" and found "Randal McGlade" on the worksheet. The next page was what we in police work call a triple I, which is a nationwide criminal justice record search through NCIC. The investigator had run this fellow, Randal McGlade. The results were negative for any record. I turned the next page, and it was a motor vehicle record on Randal.

The next part of the file had a rap sheet for Bryan Miller, and I noticed that he had been arrested on January 30, 1991, for misdemeanor theft. The next page showed arrests as a juvenile for arson in 1984, aggravated assault on June 14, 1989, curfew violation on May 15, 1987, and shoplifting on November 27, 1985.

I thought back for a moment on Richard's helix and his teachings on the progressive development of serial killers. *Arson, interesting. This guy is intriguing, but he's so young,* I thought. *And he's no military badass, that's for darn sure!*

I continued through file 668, and the next page was related to the curfew violation in 1987. The officer wrote that he had seen Bryan on a bike at 1 A.M. near 35th Avenue and Union Hills in North Phoenix. Bryan took off, and officers chased. Bryan had thrown his bike down and took off running into a backyard, where he was then apprehended.

Next, I found a stolen bicycle report that Bryan had filed on August 16, 1992. He claimed that a men's mountain bike had been stolen from his front porch at 201. E Townley.

I found a burglary report dated February 6, 1992, listing Bryan as a witness. Bryan advised that he was working as a missionary for a church and was living where the burglary occurred. The apartments were owned by the church.

I continued turning the pages of the hearty packet and located a theft report dated January 30, 1991, where Bryan had been arrested for shoplifting at a Smitty's store at 850 E. Hatcher. Bryan had removed an audio cassette, *Stick It to Ya*, from the shelves and placed it into his Walkman. When confronted by store employees and later by police, he admitted to taking the tape but said that he was going to return it on a later date.

I found another theft report dated August 16, 1990, in which Bryan shoplifted two audio cassettes—Dio's *Holy Diver* and Metallica's *Kill 'Em All*—and claimed he had no money. And yet another report from November 27, 1985, said Bryan shoplifted a small motorized speed rider toy from a grocery store in North Phoenix.

Okay, so this kid is into heavy metal and steals cassettes for his Walkman. Interesting, but savage killer? Not there yet, I thought.

Bryan Miller Stabbing

The next report shuttled me to a whole lot more interested: Bryan had been arrested on May 17, 1989. He boarded a bus in the morning in West

Phoenix, rode it to Paradise Valley Mall in northeast Phoenix, and eventually stabbed a woman named Celeste Bentley in the parking lot for no apparent reason. Bryan took off running and was later apprehended.

Wow! I thought. *Just like Angela and Melanie! Stab wound to the back.*

What I found next was nothing short of shocking. During his interview at headquarters in 1989, upon being asked about the motive for the stabbing, the officer asked him if it excited him sexually, and Bryan said no. Bryan said he did have sexual behavior problems, and that was why he had seen a doctor. When the officer asked what it felt like to stab her, Bryan told the officer, "It sent chills up my spine." Bryan also mentioned that something about the woman reminded him of his mother.

I gulped and reread Bryan's chosen words several more times. *Sent chills up his spine? Looked like his mother! Holy cow! Richard would call that a clue!* Bryan told the officers he ditched the knife. However, he later sketched the knife for the detectives, and detectives said it looked like a professional artist did it. Richard always said a lot of these guys, especially the AE subtypes, are talented in the arts—drawing, photography, painting.

The "chills up my spine" and "mother" comments churned in my mind. I turned the page and read an arson report from the Glendale Police dated March 8, 1984.

Bryan Miller Fire Setting

Bryan was eleven years old and listed as an investigative lead in the report. The fire started in a classroom wastebasket near the teacher's desk. The fire damaged the carpeting, wall, and baseboard. Bryan allegedly discovered the fire and said he had just left for the restroom. He smelled smoke and proceeded to another room to inquire about his art project. The next day Bryan admitted to arson investigators that he started the fire. When asked why he did it, Bryan said it was because of bad grades. The prior night his mother and grandmother got mad at him about bad grades. "When I got to school today, I felt like setting a fire," Bryan told them.

Okay, so we've got a troubled teenager who loves bikes, commits petty theft for audiotapes, tries to burn down his school at age eleven because he felt like it, and stabbed a woman in the back for no reason and it sent chills up his spine. I couldn't believe it . . . was this our killer?

I had to keep reading and looking at this file.

Bryan Miller Kidnapping

The next page was a report dated October 24, 1990. It was a kidnapping report listing the victim as Emma Berthier. Bryan's mother, Ellen Miller, who was listed as a detention officer for the Maricopa County Sheriff's Office in the report, brought a letter to Cactus Park Precinct in Phoenix claiming that it was Bryan's eighteenth birthday that day and he was supposed to be released from the Department of Corrections (DOC) for the aggravated assault of stabbing the woman at the mall. While Ellen was packing up his belongings from his bedroom, she found a letter describing how he was going to kidnap a girl named Emma Berthier, listed as seventeen years old.

The officers indicated that they researched the name Berthier and couldn't find anything that matched. The missing persons detail had no record, either.

The officers called the DOC and were connected to a manager at Young Acres, a halfway house. The manager said that Bryan could stay with them, as his mother did not want him living with her due to his violent behavior. The manager told officers he completed a records check on the alleged victim and found nothing. The officers stated that the report was for information only.

I read the photocopy of the letter and my hands shook.

Name: Emma Berthier   5'6" tall   17 years old

Description: Black hair, blue eyes, lightly tanned skin, 33, 25, 31

Clothing: Red blouse & skirt, black belt, red low-heel shoes, red silk lingerie with lace trim (crotchless)

Purse: Address book, wallet, pictures, make-up, $1,000 cash, keys to house & car, brush, scissors, nail clippers & long bladed knife for protection

Luggage bag: Spare clothes—1. Red black lace updress [*sic*], 1 pair gray snake print boots, 1 teal green shirt, 1 sleeveles [*sic*] sheer yarn blouse, 1 Queen Ann blouse, 3 pairs of jeans in peach, white & aqua, 1 pair hurricane washed jeans (light blue), 1 pair black moccasins, 6 pairs of red-lace panties, 4 pair of red lace bras, 1 denim jacket, 1 razor for shaving her legs, hair mousse

My Equipment:
1 roll of masking tape, 1 long blade knife, 1 carving fork, 1 carving knife, 1 large liquid container to hold blood, 1 large garbage bag to hold body parts, video camera, gloves, black hood, black jacket, shirt & pants, camera, 4 pairs of handcuffs, 5 pieces of long rope, BBQ grill, seasonings, supercharged Dodge 4WD pickup with camper top, lantern, matches, combat boots, police & emergency radio, cooking pan, extra clothes, hacksaw, 22 semi-automatic handgun.

Plan:

Videotape

Kidnap the girl

Tie her up to the truck

Cut her clothes off

Fuck her

Lick all of her body

Search through her personals.

Shave her pussy

Fuck her again

Fell [*sic*] her titts [*sic*] & suck on them

Stick my tongue in her pussy and lick it to get her excited.

Bite one of her nipples off

Punch her a few times

Stick my fist into her pussy

Fuck her in the ass

Take pictures of her

Pull out pans, knives, fork, bag, grill, Hacksaw & seasonings

Give her some small cuts to scare her

Stick the fork into her leg and start carving

Cut off the bone with the hacksaw

Pour the blood into liquid container

Kill her by slicing open her belly and pulling out her organs

Fire up the BBQ and start cooking her body parts to eat

Preserve the head, titts, and pussy so I can look at them whenever I want.

The detective assigned to this case in November 1990 wrote that the elements of the crime of kidnapping were not present, and the officer took it for informational purposes. The detective continued, "The letter seems to detail a possible fantasy including eating and saving certain body parts." The detective said he reached out to the location where Bryan had been incarcerated. The probation officer said that a therapist believed Bryan Miller was dangerous and tried to get him into a treatment facility after being released from custody. The therapist, however, believed the letter was just a fantasy. The detective added a supplement to his report after the therapist called him. The therapist said he had confronted Bryan about the letter, and Bryan said that he would fantasize and pull names out of magazines. The therapist told the detective that Bryan was "not dangerous."

Not dangerous! What do you mean, "not dangerous"? He just stabbed a woman in the back who reminded him of his mother, which sent chills up his spine! I thought. *This is textbook serial killer stuff, and Richard would wholeheartedly agree.* My gut told me that this was quite possibly our killer, but we had been excited about different leads so many times before only to be told by Kelley and the lab over and over, "He's been ruled out." This guy looked really good. *Would the theory hold true?* I had to brief my squad, and soon.

Victim #1 Angela Brosso

Victim #2 Melanie Bernas

Map of crime scenes

Aerial view of Angela's crime scene and apartment complex

Discovery of Angela's head in the canal

Drag marks from bike trail at Angela's crime scene

Aerial View of Melanie's crime scene

Drag marks towards canal at Melanie's crime scene

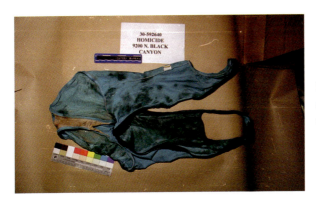

Bodysuit the killer redressed Melanie in after the initial attack

Tunnel art near Melanie's crime scene

CRIME INFORMATION BULLETIN

PHOENIX POLICE DEPARTMENT
DENNIS A. GARRETT, POLICE CHIEF
620 W. WASHINGTON ST
PHOENIX, ARIZONA 85003

GENERAL INVESTIGATIONS BUREAU

HOMICIDE DETAIL

THIS IS A REQUEST FOR YOUR ASSISTANCE

MISSING BICYCLE BELONGS TO HOMICIDE VICTIM

DIAMOND BACK "TOPANGA" MOUNTAIN BIKE - PURPLE

STANDARD BIKE SEAT - 18" MEN'S FRAME - 26" WHEELS

21 GEAR SPEED - WHITE PLASTIC WATER BOTTLE WITH DIAMOND BACK LOGO

Additional information on file in Homicide Detail

If you have seen this bicycle or may have information as to it's location, please contact the Phoenix Police Department Homicide Detail.

Homicide Detail:	495-5883
Silent Witness:	261-8600
Homicide Hotline:	256-3212

Crime bulletin depicting Angela's missing bicycle

CRIME INFORMATION BULLETIN

PHOENIX POLICE DEPARTMENT
DENNIS A. GARRETT, POLICE CHIEF
620 W. WASHINGTON ST
PHOENIX, ARIZONA 85003

GENERAL INVESTIGATIONS BUREAU
HOMICIDE DETAIL

THIS IS A REQUEST FOR YOUR ASSISTANCE

MISSING BICYCLE BELONGS TO HOMICIDE VICTIM

SPECIALIZED HARD ROCK SPORT 1992, 21 SPEED BOYS BIKE
GREEN IN FRONT, BLUE IN BACK
CHROME WATER BOTTLE MOUNT ON LOWER BAR

Additional information on file in Homicide Detail

If you have seen this bicycle or may have information as to it's location,
please contact the Phoenix Police Department Homicide Detail.

Homicide Detail: 262-6141
Silent Witness: 261-8600

Crime bulletin depicting Melanie's missing bicycle

Trip to Vidocq Society in Philadelphia, PA in 2013:
William Schira, Ken Pollock, William Fleisher,
Marianne Ramirez, and Troy Hillman (left to right)

TOP LEFT: Bryan Patrick Miller, early 1990's, around the time of the murders

CENTER AND BOTTOM BELOW: Bryan Patrick Miller in Zombie Hunter attire circa 2015

ABOVE: Zombie Hunter car driven by Bryan Patrick Miller at time of arrest
BELOW: Bryan Patrick Miller's kitchen at the time
of the arrest in 2015 with artwork on refrigerator

CHAPTER 19
THE LASER FOCUS ON FILE 668

T he cold case work area buzzed with activity. The elite team worked tirelessly doing what they did best: They investigated. It was like a finely tuned orchestra. In no time, the deep-dive examination and collaboration were complete. We didn't know everything about Bryan Patrick Miller, but the latest discoveries beyond file 668 were invaluable. Bryan drove a car that he referred to as the "Zombie Hunter." There was a still shot of a YouTube page that read, "AZ Zombie Hunter Crown Vic." We also saw a photo of Bryan in a military-style outfit with a large gun over his shoulder. He bought the Crown Vic at a police auction and converted it. *Pure fantasy.*

It was clear he knew a ton about cars from his YouTube description: "low RPM, 2007 Crown Victoria P71 chambered mufflers, headers, TF heads, stage 2 cams." Bryan had multiple YouTube videos in which he drove another car around some type of track. We found several recent reports of him being stopped in the Crown Victoria by patrol officers. The officers described the car, saying that Bryan had it all set up like a real patrol car.

One of the reports in the packet detailed a traffic stop on November 26, 2014, close to where Melanie was killed. The officer wrote, "While driving S/B on I-17 from Northern observed listed vehicle. Vehicle is a Crown Vic and is made to look like a police car had yellow and blue lights on top. Red/white bars in the rear behind the other lights. And a star on the driver door.

Rear of car said Zombie Patrol. No crime. Done for documentation in case vehicle is ever used to pull over citizens. Male driver."

A second report dated May 30, 2014, detailed another stop at a location near our murders. The officer wrote, "S1 [Bryan Miller] has a Ford Crown Victoria with green and yellow lights mounted to the top of the vehicle. S1 has a computer set up like police, has handcuffs, and a pellet rifle. S1 vehicle states Zombie Hunter on the rear. S1 was in the neighborhood moving a friend."

The fine details of this man took form, and a timeline developed—a timeline tightly woven around our murder locations. Bryan currently lived in central Phoenix, and he worked at an Amazon distribution facility in West Phoenix. He grew up in a house just north and west of Angela's murder in Phoenix, so one could surmise he knew the area well. Just before the first murder took place in August 1992, he lived in an apartment in central Phoenix not too far from the murder scenes. He lived at another address, also relatively close, in central Phoenix in 1994. He lived in the State of Washington from 1997 through about 2002, and then he moved to his current house in Phoenix. We clearly placed him in Phoenix during the times of both our murders.

His mother was Martha "Ellen" Miller, who died in December 2010. Bryan was an only child and born in Michigan. His father, Lester Miller, was in the Army and stationed in Hawaii. At age five, Bryan lost his dad to a motorcycle accident. Bryan's mother moved to Phoenix when Bryan was seven to be closer to her parents, Lela and David James. David passed in February 1994. Lela died in October 2010.

Bryan married Amy Miller in the late 1990s; they divorced in the mid-2000s. They lived in Washington during most of that time. Bryan had a fifteen-year-old daughter named Sarah. She was apparently living with him.

In addition to the reports in file 668, we found an aggravated assault report from October 1994, where Bryan claimed that he was riding his bike home from work at St. Vincent de Paul and was almost run over by a vehicle. It was a month after Melanie was killed in 1994.

Richard would say that was a sarcastic ruse, I thought. Bryan was also arrested for assault with a weapon in 2002 in Everett, Washington. He was found not guilty.

We also located his LinkedIn site, where he described his current work at Amazon as a contractor for Integrity Staffing Solutions. He also described manufacturing aluminum truck canopies in Washington. Bryan referenced a multiday event as a director for Old Tucson Studios and photo booth staff at Phoenix Comic Con, an event where the focus is on comic books and related culture. People dress up like comic book characters. He also stated that he had done set production and casting for a web series I hadn't heard of. We researched it and found that it was based on a science fiction theme. He worked security at St. Vincent De Paul and was also an electronics and pharmacy associate at Walmart. He worked briefly at McDonald's.

His Facebook page was, likewise, intriguing. His profile picture was a masked person with a helmet who looked like something out of *Star Wars*, and there was another smaller picture of a person wearing a trench coat and carrying a large gun. He called himself Hwyaden Lwcus, which were Welsh words translated into "lucky duck." His email address started with "theduck13." We also found a ton of pictures where Bryan was dressed up in steampunk attire with guns in some type of futuristic yet Old West–style shootout. We looked it up, and steampunk is a type of science fiction with a historical element. People dress in costumes and act out fictional scenes. In one of the pictures, Bryan had a huge old clock necklace hung around his neck and a leather helmet with the Eiffel Tower on it. *More fantasy.*

The next page was an IMDb biography, which is for the movie industry. Bryan claimed he was born in Trenton, Michigan, with nicknames of "the Duck," "Lucky Duck" and "Hwyaden Lwcus." He was listed as an actor in

Mantecoza (2014). The movie description read: "Sebastian King, an average office worker, is suddenly thrust into the steampunk world of Mantecoza where he struggles to learn how to be a Wizard."

We located links on his pages and YouTube uploads referencing St. Maria Goretti. She was a young Catholic girl from Italy who, one day, was attacked by a neighbor and told him that she would rather die than submit. The neighbor stabbed her with a knife a total of fourteen times. She forgave this neighbor for his actions on her deathbed. This neighbor dreamt of her after three years in prison and repented his life of crime. Maria was later canonized for her purity as a model for youth by the pope. Today, she serves as the patron saint of youth, young women, and victims of rape.

We also found hyperlinks to clips of a cartoon girl named Lenore, the Cute Little Dead Girl. This cartoon was done by a man named Roman Dirge. In reading up on Dirge, he is an artist, magician, and creepy comic writer. His works include *Lenore*, *The Monsters in My Tummy*, and *It Ate Billy on Christmas*. The character Lenore was a creation of Edgar Allan Poe in a poem in the mid-1800s. She was a beautiful woman who died at a young age. There was reference to people meeting in paradise in the afterlife. We watched a host of *Lenore, the Cute Little Dead Girl* animated shorts that Bryan had highlighted. There was one where she randomly kills a bunch of hamsters at a pet store. When Lenore tells the store manager, he looks and vomits.

We discovered a picture of Bryan Miller when he was eighteen. We wondered how this skinny little kid could drag two athletically built women for hundreds of feet. He was not the military badass we had conjured. *Ugh! Maybe this isn't our guy? Or did anger for his mother fuel his rage?* We had all heard of stories of enormous feats of strength during moments of high emotion. *Keep calm. The DNA would be the key.*

At the end of the great collaboration, I told the team, "Great work! Now, let's figure out a plan to get his DNA. Oh, and remember to keep a lid on this guy until we have him ruled in or out, please."

⌒

I thought about Bryan and his rather bizarre and interesting nickname, Hwyaden Lwcus, which we had determined was Welsh. I pondered a possible connection with the carvings, tunnel writings, and religious symbolism in our murders to this Welsh fascination. I found a Welsh story about St. Winifred's well. It was about a young prince named Caradoc, who had seen a young girl named Winifred. According to the story, Caradoc came on to Winifred, and she rejected him, running toward the church. Caradoc then felt mistreated, chased her down, and cut her head off with a sword. The head rolled down a hill near the church, where Winifred's father saw it, wrapped it in his cloak, and returned it to the church. The father requested prayers and reattached the head to the body. When Winifred came to, she had only a threadlike red mark around her throat. The fountain nearby was allegedly stained with her blood.

I found this possible connection a bit chilling. We had a rejected suitor (Caradoc) who cut off the head of a woman (Winifred). We had the overall church symbolism. Not to mention we had found a very thin but continuous laceration on the neck of the second victim, Melanie. It was unsettling.

I was hooked on the research and frantically searched "Caradoc" for more information. *What if Bryan thought of himself as this Caradoc fellow,* I thought? I found that Caradoc was sometimes referred to as Caradog, and that St. Winifred was the patron saint of virgins. *Wow!* I thought, *the beheaded patron saint of virgins—how intriguing!* I read that St. Winifred had been depicted in various forms of art carrying her head in her hands. *This will be one hell of a story if it's him.*

CHAPTER 20
THE RUSE

The Zombie Hunter car lurched into the Chili's parking lot. We sat at a large table in the corner with a clear view of the parking lot, the entry door, and the reserved table. I was a bundle of nerves. Any other Friday afternoon would call for beer and boneless wings. I could even smell the wings from the kitchen. However, I was laser focused on the task at hand. We had one shot to get this right. We needed to go undetected and get what we came for.

Bryan Miller got out of the car. He looked normal and could easily blend into any crowd. *Ted Bundy looked normal too, though*, I thought. Bryan was dressed in a simple pair of jeans and a T-shirt—not typical job interview attire.

Something was wrong. There was a teenage girl with him. Whispers broke out at our table.

"Who's that?" Mark said.

"His daughter," said JJ.

"Was he supposed to bring her to the interview?" asked Dom.

"Clark didn't say anything about it. It was supposed to be just Bryan," I said.

Clark had approached Bryan the week before in the parking lot of Amazon's distribution facility. Clark noticed that Bryan sat in the Zombie Hunter on every break. Bryan did not smoke or litter. After a week of intense surveillance, discarded DNA was not an option. We needed his DNA. Clark's plan was implemented. Posing as the security manager for a business next to Amazon that had been the target of a rash of employee theft, Clark said he needed a security worker to watch the parking lot for suspicious activity. Bryan took the bait.

Clark walked up to Bryan near the hostess area. Bryan introduced the teenage girl to Clark. The hostess then guided them to the table. My heart thundered, and I tried not to stare. Undercover work was not in my wheelhouse.

The table in the corner was carefully selected and reserved by the team hours before. Dom and JJ met with the Chili's manager that morning. Thankfully, her father was a retired officer, and we received red-carpet treatment. She was a huge help with the setup of the isolated table, which included extra-sanitized utensils.

Bryan's daughter sat to his right, and he sat directly across from Clark. We faced Clark and watched Bryan's movements. We focused on his utensils. These were the DNA honeypot.

Clark explained the job offer and did most of the talking for the next half hour. Bryan focused most of his attention on his burger and fries. His daughter appeared equally silent.

Clark, Bryan, and the girl got up and headed for the door. We sprang into action.

JJ and Dom quickly pulled on gloves to avoid contamination.

"The girl sat to Bryan's right. Let's mark the fork, knife, cup, and straw separately for that area," Dom said.

"How are we supposed to get the liquid out of the cup without washing away any DNA evidence," asked JJ.

"Good question. Just do the best you can," I replied.

"Drill a hole in the bottom, maybe?" said a member of the team.

"That would work, but I don't have my DeWalt handy," said JJ.

JJ came up with a quick way to discard the liquid without destroying any possible saliva. We collected all the silverware, glasses, and straws and waited inside until we got the text from Clark that Bryan had driven away.

We met up with Clark outside his truck. I think we were all relieved, yet worried that we didn't get a good sample of his DNA.

"Was that his daughter? What the hell did he bring her for?" I asked.

Clark shook his head. "Yes, and I have no idea. He didn't say anything about bringing her. That just messed things all up. To make matters worse, the guy ate a whole sandwich and a host of fries and didn't take a single drink until the very end. Who does that?"

"The good thing is that we collected everything. I hope the lab can get something," I said.

"Do you think he figured it out?" asked JJ.

Clark shook his head and replied, "I don't think so. He seemed excited about the security job. I told him that I would be in touch after the background check. He didn't flinch at that."

We all drove away, and I called Kelley to give her the heads-up. She promised to process it quickly.

I churned over all the information in the file and collected by the team on Bryan Miller. I thought about the plain man I just saw at Chili's. *He's definitely not Rambo.*

CHAPTER 21
THE ONE

The heavy wooden door to the conference room burst open. We tried to process the sheer rudeness and unprofessional nature of the intrusion. It was Kelley and her DNA team, and the scientists never came over to headquarters. Their building was much newer and nicer.

Kelley said, "Sorry! But we wanted to let you know in person that *you did it*! Bryan Miller's DNA matches! Congratulations!"

The silence in the room was deafening. It was like a bunch of fatigued soldiers hearing the news that an endless war was over, and they could finally go home to their loved ones. Indeed, they heard the words, but they didn't trust the words. A pervading mental survival and coping shield guarded them.

Dazed myself, I finally mustered some words. "You're kidding, right? You know it's not nice to play games. We can only take so much disappointment."

Kelley retorted, "No, no, *you got him!* I told you that's the way these cases would get solved. You had to give us the right DNA!"

The words finally permeated, and everybody stood up and embraced in a group hug fueled by raw human emotion and cheer. It was a genuine happiness for these two beautiful, savagely murdered women who had been cheated of their lives and for their loved ones finally getting the justice they so well deserved. After three and a half painstaking years of disappointment stacked upon disappointment, we had finally located the missing puzzle piece in the investigation. I was lightheaded and shell-shocked. From the looks on the faces of the rest of the squad, they were, too. Relief and glee overpowered the room, for the moment at least, but the celebration was fleeting. We needed to get this maggot in custody and search his Zombie Hunter car and house ASAP.

"I've got to grab the lieutenant," I stammered to the team. "Marianne, please call Bob Shutts over at the county attorney's office and let him know. Bob was the prosecutor who went out to the original crime scenes and had followed the cases for years. We need him involved. Kelley, who else knows about this?"

Kelley replied, "My staff, and now you guys."

I looked at the team and tried to reel in my thoughts. "Okay, not a word of it gets out until we get him, okay, everybody?" I knew this would be a massive arrest for the department, media, and community, and we couldn't afford to tip him off.

Still dazed, I jogged to my boss's office and told him about the DNA match. He was shocked.

We toggled from short-lived joyfulness to a let's-get-this-asshole planning phase. We all knew the war was not won. In less than an hour, the conference room buzzed with the higher-ups and interested parties from all sections of the department. Apprehension was the next phase, and in that vein, we launched a meeting with the heads of our tactical teams. The SAU and Fugitive Apprehension lieutenants were briefed on the details we had so far on Bryan Miller, and the department now had the top research analysts working on this case. The plan was to send out several SAU and Fugitive Apprehension squads to apprehend Bryan at work, grab the Zombie Hunter car, and safely secure his home with search warrants. The Homicide unit would take it from there.

After the tactical briefing, I called a quick squad meeting in a small conference room. I said, "Well, holy cow, team, we did it! A three-and-a-half-year-long journey, and we somehow connected the dots, even though everyone kept telling us he was dead and we were wasting our time. I'm *so proud of you!* As you can probably imagine, the next few days, weeks, and months are going to be hellaciously busy. We have only started. It's imperative that we dot our *i*'s and cross our *t*'s to make sure this maggot never sees the light of day again. I'm gonna break down the assignments. Okay?"

I rattled off assignments. William would interview Bryan after SAU and Fugitive Apprehension picked him up. Dom would draft the search warrants with the help of JJ. Marianne would interview Bryan's daughter, Sarah, and his best friend, Randal "Randy" McGlade. Clark would interview Bryan's ex-wife, Amy. Mark would stick with me to take notes and figure out how to handle all the incoming calls from other agencies and the community. I would get word to Angela's and Melanie's families.

The team split off like worker ants in the colony and focused on their assigned tasks. I managed to call Karyn to let her know the news before things blossomed even further.

"Hi, beautiful, so, you remember the Zombie Hunter guy? Well, we just found out from the lab that he's the canal killer! Can you believe that? We got him!"

"Wow, that's unbelievable, babe! Yay! You guys did it! I knew you would! Congratulations!"

"Thanks! I've got to go but two things really quick—one, I obviously won't be home for dinner or for quite some time, for that matter, as we have tons to do, and two, please don't tell a soul, as we don't want the media involved until we get him in custody and everything secure."

"No problem. I'm so happy for you guys! Love you!"

Now I need to bear down and focus, I thought. So much could still go wrong. Bryan Miller could suddenly flee the area and end up in another country with a long extradition period. . . He could destroy key pieces of evidence at his house prior to our arrival. Bryan could also erase incriminating digital evidence on his computers and phone. I made my way back to the conference room and met the lead prosecutor for all cold cases from the Maricopa County Attorney's Office, Bob Shutts. Many a defense attorney feared him. He had periodically monitored our progress on the canal murders because he was a newer prosecutor when Angela and Melanie were murdered and always took a strong interest in the cases.

I received a phone call from William around 6:00 P.M.

"Good news. Bryan is in custody. The managers called him into the main office and SAU and Fugitive Apprehension took him down without a hitch."

I smiled and replied, "Excellent! What about the Zombie Hunter car?"

"It's been seized, and we're getting it towed to the yard. The only other thing is he's got a locker at the facility. Security here searched it already, and they're gonna turn over the contents. There's nothing of evidentiary value, though."

"Okay, great! Was he surprised?"

William responded, "Yeah, they said he looked frightened."

"He should be! You good with interviewing him?"

"I've got it, boss man!"

JJ called me and told me SAU had breached Bryan's house. The only person home was his daughter, Sarah. SAU attempted to clear the house, but Bryan was a hoarder.

"There's stuff stacked almost to the ceiling. Frankly, boss, this is a shithole, and it smells god-awful. We could be out here weeks, if not months," JJ said.

I told him we would get him some help at the house. I briefed the lieutenant on the condition of Bryan's house. Without hesitation, he picked up his phone and deployed a very seasoned and thorough homicide sergeant to lead the house search warrant and collection of evidence. That sergeant quickly assembled a team of volunteer detectives to work that angle, including JJ, Dom, and Clark. Mark, William, and Marianne worked out of the war room and organized all the anticipated tips and calls coming in from the public, law enforcement agencies, and so on.

There was so much to do. Sleep would have to wait.

CHAPTER 22
THE INTERVIEW

The shell of the man seemed calm. The telltale visual indicators detectives are taught to extract from perpetrators before interrogation were absent. No sweat. No fidgety hands. No toe taps. No heavy breathing. Nothing. Yet, on the inside of this cloaked man, we can only imagine that panic gripped him. For more than twenty years, he had eluded this very moment. He now glimpsed his fate in the executioner's room and the unforgiving needle that would deliver the final blow to his mortal body. The end of the road for Bryan Patrick Miller. Or, on the other hand, perhaps he soothed his anxiety with thoughts of police ineptitude. He was of superior intelligence, after all. The fools undoubtedly had botched something. He just needed to spar with the weak adversary to figure out what. He beat them in Washington to reclaim his freedom; he could do it again.

I studied the man on the live feed television screen from the conference room. I tried to decipher him visually. He was like the uninspiring cover of a book. The military badass I had conjured was not there, and I wanted to dissect him further. Men killed for reasons like war and self-preservation. This man killed for nothing more than pleasure. I yearned for a tour inside his twisted mind. *Would he let us in? Or would he wall off his prized secrets?* I hoped he would embark on a tell-all rant in hopes for leniency. It could go either way. William would steer the interview, but sadly Bryan would ultimately control it.

Five minutes prior, the conference room had been an ant farm of activity. Now, the room seemed more like a morgue. Eyes and ears were fixated on the large television. Every word held decades of importance.

ॐ

I pulled out my notes from a few years ago. I had so many questions both then and now for this man. Attempt after attempt was made to unlock his clever clues, but the answers eluded us. If the serial killer began to spew, I prayed these glaring potholes of questions would be filled in.

- Why did the killer write *WSC* in dark red (blood/marker/ paint?) on tunnel wall? (Melanie's murder)—three places of *WSC*—body, sign, and tunnel wall—major clue?
- Why did he write *Tweety*? What does it mean?
- What is the relevance of the man in the fedora?
- Any meaning to other markings of *KAW*, *Blitz*, or *Little Devil*?
- Why did the killer take Angela's head and later place it back in the water? Both scenes involved water—why did he deliberately drag Melanie into the water, risking getting caught? Why did he re-dress her in a young girl's swimsuit? what's the fascination? WATER—why, why, why?
- Why did the killer use/choose areas near tunnels? Graffiti in tunnel with Melanie and re-dress near tunnel; pedestrian tunnel nearby with Angela. Why?
- Why did he cut their clothing with a knife?
- Why did he leave their shoes and socks on?
- Why did the killer position Angela with her feet to the east? (Possible religious meaning?)
- Why did the killer carve *WSC* between Melanie's breasts? What does it mean?

- Why did he carve a cross with three dots below the *WSC* on Melanie? Why three dots on a cross—meaning?
- Religious significance of cutting on Angela? Two round holes in lower midsection; transection of body—cut like cross? Religion again?
- Why did killer paint/mark a sign near Melanie's scene *93 WSC*?

We knew what happened to those girls. We didn't know how or why or who else he might have harmed or killed. The man seated before us could fill in all those blanks.

It would not be easy. Richard forewarned the group that this "chap" would "jest" with us. It was part of a one-sided, amusing game for this Jeffrey Dahmer type. Richard's words entered my mind: "Dear boy, they think they are unequivocally smarter than the rest of us. Do not underestimate them." I had faith in William. William was clever. People naturally liked him. He had a method for gaining trust and then extracting information. This would be a vicious chess match.

William entered the room. He sat directly across from Bryan with nothing more than a small table separating good and evil. The tiny sterile room welcomed an epic battle—a mental boxing match. *Here we go!* I twirled my pen to relieve my bubbling anxiousness. I pined for a full confession yet feared a complete shutdown. We had him nailed on the DNA, but his statements would secure the investigation. Unlike me, William matched Bryan with outward calmness. William wasted no time and launched into the warm-up phase. Bryan's standard rights had been read, so the games could begin. William probed with benign background questions. I breathed a sigh of relief. Bryan could have invoked his rights at this point, but he didn't. He wanted to play.

Bryan spoke freely. He told William he was born in Michigan and went with his parents to Hawaii due to his father being in the Army, and they stayed there for about ten years. He didn't know a lot about his father but said he was special forces. Bryan came back to North Phoenix and moved in with his grandmother. His mom later joined them. She worked as security at a grocery store in Hawaii before they moved back. Bryan was picked on a lot as a kid because he didn't like sports. His uncle taught him martial arts, but he wouldn't elaborate. *So far, so good*, I thought.

William steered Bryan to the subject of bikes and a known comfort zone. Bryan lit up and spilled information. He had collected them and told William about his BMX, choppers, beachcombers, and mountain bikes. He had a Mongoose mountain bike. He rode his bikes extensively.

William wrote quickly in his notepad and would only afford Bryan an occasional glance up. Our conference room remained like a library. William veered Bryan to the topic of religion. Bryan's mother was Mormon, but he attended a nondenominational church. His grandparents weren't churchgoers but had connections to the Mennonite church. Bryan started with the Mennonite church in the early 1990s.

I grabbed my phone and searched the Mennonite church. An entry indicated they were "Anabaptists." I didn't know what that meant. The entry compared them to the Amish, who lived simple lives. *Now, I understand.*

Bryan took a quick right turn from religion to his mom beating him on a regular basis. She beat him with her security belt, which had a particularly nasty buckle. This all started when he was five after his father died. The schoolteachers and nurses all saw the welts but did nothing. Nobody would believe him because his mother was connected to law enforcement. She was a detention officer with the county sheriff's office. *Did his anger toward women start here? Is he setting up the "poor Bryan" defense?*

William obliged and followed Bryan to his criminal background. He admitted to shoplifting, criminal damage, and the assault. When William explored the assault at Paradise Valley Mall, where he stabbed a woman in the back, Bryan stated he "kinda blacked out." The woman looked a lot like his mom. He said, "That's totally not me." He "lived in fear." This was a reference to his mother. Bryan drew pictures to deal with all of it. *He just built part of his defense*, I thought. *He was the victim.*

William slid the fantasy letter his mother turned in to police when he was eighteen across the table. The letter was in his file and etched in our minds. It described in horrid detail the kidnap, torture, and murder of a young woman. Bryan looked at the letter and told William it didn't look familiar. However, it looked like his handwriting. It was something from a movie. His mother liked horror movies.

William guided Bryan to the topic of where in the area he rode his bike. He stuck to the Metrocenter and Sunnyslope area. He denied rides on the canals, tunnels, and bike paths. Bryan threw in that he may have taken the bike paths at night once but didn't like it. They scared him, and that's why he didn't take them. *Sarcastic ruse. They didn't scare him; rather, they invigorated him. Richard would be entertained by that statement.*

When William directed the questions toward sex acts and masturbation, Bryan denied masturbating in public. Then, he abruptly diverted to "It's possible a few times." He claimed that he had only had sex one time back then with a "Mexican" prostitute at age eighteen. He never had sex or masturbated near the bike paths. When asked about sex or masturbation on the canals, Bryan said, "Not that I recall." When William asked him about sex with girls on bike paths, he responded that he wished he had met girls out there. He denied any sexual assaults or stabbing anyone besides the girl at Paradise Valley Mall. He also denied dressing up in women's clothes. *He just dropped another sarcastic ruse. He did meet girls out there. They just didn't want to meet him.*

William swooped closer to the details of our murders. He began to press Bryan on specifics. *This is it. Drumroll for the tell-all confession.* My heart had to be at two hundred beats per minute at this point. I needed to calm down, but this was just too much. *We are close.* Bryan suddenly walled up and denied knowing Angela or Melanie. He declared that he "had no clue" who they were. William pushed him on why his DNA was associated with them. Bryan deflected that he "didn't see how that was possible. Can't explain DNA, can't remember everything I did back then, didn't kill anyone." Bryan repeated these statements and dug in.

Bryan downshifted to shame and embarrassment when he hired prostitutes around Van Buren and Camelback. *Deflection*, I thought. William brought him back to the murders and his DNA. Bryan doubled down: "It's impossible . . . never had sex on a bike path . . . everyone I had sex with is still alive."

William got up and left the room, a tactic used by seasoned veterans to let the perpetrator stew. He would break him down in a methodical manner. Bryan blurted that the interrogation was a "frickin' nightmare," and "Why is this fucking happening to me?"

William returned to the taxing chess game. In a calculated manner, he started in on Bryan about weapons. Bryan denied he carried weapons. His shields were up. William asked about the knife used in the Paradise Valley Mall attack. Bryan did an about-face and said back then he was scared at school and carried one for protection.

William probed toward another area. St. Maria Goretti, the patron saint of virgins, on his YouTube account was brought up. Bryan said, "I wasn't in church for her." *Strange answer.*

William shifted back to the bike paths. Bryan said he wouldn't bike near the tunnels and canals. They were "dark," he was "vulnerable," and he had a "fear of people." I slammed my fist, shattering the silence in the conference room, and yelled out, "Bullshit!" Bryan added that he leaves conflict when it unfolds around him.

William returned to a benign spot. He asked Bryan why he was fascinated with ducks. He said that in grade school he used to quack like a duck. His nickname Hwyaden Lwcus is Welsh for "lucky duck."

William threw jabs at this point instead of a knockout punch and took Bryan to another comfort zone: cars. Bryan spoke freely and rattled off a ton of stuff about them. He then got into his adventures in steampunk, diesel punk, comic cons, and the zombie stuff. Bryan was in his fantasy land now and spouted off freely. He went to a zombie walk wearing a gas mask and a trench coat, carrying a Nerf gun. This is where the whole Zombie Hunter car idea developed. *Pure fantasy. Tell us more, Bryan.*

William left the room again to allow Bryan to stew and to confer with Clark on the phone. When he reentered, he jabbed Bryan on violence with his ex-wife. Bryan told him it was light bondage, which he thought was normal. He admitted to holding a knife to her throat but said it was all fun. They did do some "bloodletting." William pounced on the bloodletting comment and started his mighty right hook. Bryan knocked the pieces off the chess board and invoked his right to an attorney. For the first time, I saw William abandon his poker face. He had almost broken the barrier. William got up, stretched his back, and left the room.

I rubbed my brow and squinted. It was all over. No tell-all confession. A denial would still work for the prosecution, but we wanted to know so much more.

We heard Bryan fuming inside the room. "This is complete bullshit. I didn't kill anyone. Why would she say that? Why does she hate me so much? I can't even stand the sight of blood. All those people working in my head. Why is the world always gonna screw with me? Where the hell did they get my DNA? This is all bullshit." He added that his ex-wife wanted him to "punish" her.

Mark said, "Wait! *He* couldn't stand the sight of blood? Didn't he brag in his letter about bringing buckets for the blood?"

I said, "Yeah, it's his sarcastic irony. Blood turns him on. Richard would love these comments."

William was upset at himself. I told him I was impressed he had just gone toe-to-toe with a serial killer. We all knew this was not a typical interview, and no ordinary detective could have sparred with him. Bryan was one of Richard's prized anger-excitation subtypes. I reminded William of what the prophetic profiler had told me: These subtypes had higher-than-average

IQs and were extremely difficult to interview. They played coy and wanted to flip the interview to figure out what the police had on them. In fact, these interviews were nothing more than a game to them.

Bryan was transported in handcuffs and shackles to the Maricopa County Jail by a team of highly trained tactical officers. Indeed, Bryan was not the military badass we conjured up on our journey, but his propensity for violence could not be disregarded. We could not allow this killer back on the streets.

CHAPTER 23
THE EX-WIFE AND THE BEST FRIEND

Bryan was in his late teens and lived alone in an apartment near 2nd Street and Dunlap. A man from his church had given him the apartment. A teenage Girl Scout came to his door with her parents to sell cookies, but he did not order any. She was a special needs girl. A week or so later, she mistakenly went to Bryan's door to drop off cookies. No one was with her this time. He yanked her inside, slit her throat, put her in his bathtub, and chopped her up into pieces. In his state of excitement, he made a mistake and ran warm water instead of cold. He wanted the body to stay intact longer. Warm water would accelerate the decomposition. The daily experimentation and fantasy of it all would end much sooner than he wanted. He had to throw her away in the trash, as the stench would bring attention to his apartment.

Bryan confessed these chilling details to Amy during their marriage. Amy had held the story in until now. Clark didn't blink an eye. He knew this matched up with an open missing child case, that of Brandy Myers. A few details were different, but it generally matched. It took place before Angela's murder in 1992.

We knew that Bryan and Amy divorced in 2006. We also had discovered that it was a contentious divorce and lasted for quite some time. We hoped the fury and scorn from Amy would induce her to give us the details we craved on the killer she had once loved.

Amy told Clark the two met at St. Vincent de Paul in approximately 1995. She was a volunteer, and her aunt worked there. Bryan worked there, operating the printing press. Their first date was at Castles and Coasters, an amusement park that overlooked the scene of Melanie's attack in 1993. They got married in August 1997, and the next year, they moved to Everett, Washington, and lived with Bryan's mother and her cousin. Bryan told her that his mother was horrible, yet when they were together, they acted like they adored each other. Amy said she found that strange. She also said the relationship between his mom and cousin was odd, and it seemed like they were in a relationship.

Amy continued divulging to Clark. When Bryan was ten, his mother threatened to cut off his penis because he had been messing around with her makeup. She claimed Bryan told her that his mother was physically abusive. Amy reaffirmed that Bryan's real father died when he was five. Bryan told her that she was his first girlfriend, and the first girl he had ever kissed. She described him during the courtship and early marriage as quiet, shy, polite, and lazy. She said that things changed in Washington after his arrest for assault.

Bryan told Amy that the victim in Washington was a prostitute who came to his work after hours wanting to use the phone. She then attacked him. The woman's version was that he had picked her up and taken her to his workplace when no one was around. She had picked up the phone, and he blitz attacked, stabbing her in the back. The woman was still able to fight back, and she ran to a neighbor's house to call police.

Amy told me that Bryan never really talked about what he did as a juvenile to get in trouble. He told her that he had ridden the bus to Paradise Valley Mall and stabbed a woman in the back because she resembled his mother.

Amy had grown up very religious and was taught that a wife does whatever her husband wants. She had found his pornography collection, which was mostly just *Playboys*, before he went to jail. When he got back, he began to show her his computer. She described seeing both photos and videos of men killing women, cutting throats, boiling body parts, and eating them. Bryan would randomly show them to her. The concept of sexual interest in a woman and wanting to kill her was intermingled in his mind. He preferred redheads and girls around fourteen years old who were just starting to develop.

During sex, Bryan would tie Amy up, hold a knife to her throat, make small cuts on her breasts, and lick the blood. Amy said that he never cut her vagina, but he would take straight pins and push them into her breasts, mouth, and genitalia. Amy said that it wasn't a wife's place to say no. She was afraid for her life, and Bryan told her that if he didn't love her so much, he would have killed her.

Amy described one time when he had his knife during sex and grabbed her ponytail and cut it off. Bryan also told her that he wanted to watch her have sex with another person, male or female. They ended up getting a divorce in 2006, when she left him for another man.

Clark asked her why she didn't report the Girl Scout story to the police. She told him she didn't think she had enough information and that she was scared. She wasn't sure if he was capable of doing it.

Amy described Bryan as a manipulative person and pathological liar. He spent all his time on the computer or watching TV. He acted like he was religious initially, and that all changed after he got out of jail in Washington. He told Amy that he used to hire prostitutes before meeting her. He biked up and down the canal all the time when they lived in Phoenix. He would ride his bike to her house near 36th Avenue and Cactus when they were dating.

Amy told Clark that Bryan told her about another attack in Washington before the one in 2002. He didn't get caught on that one, either. Apparently, there was a trail near their apartment. One morning, a young girl was walking to school, and he attacked her with a knife. She was hurt but survived. The police somehow got it wrong that the perp had tattoos on his arms, and Bryan had no tattoos. Bryan also cut his hair and shaved immediately after the attack to avoid detection.

✑

Marianne was a forensic interviewer and had vast training in interviewing children. She interviewed Bryan's daughter, Sarah, after we made the arrest. Sarah told Marianne that she got along fine with both her mother and father. She lived with her father and claimed there was no physical, mental, or sexual abuse; he would only yell when he got upset. Sarah was very fond of one of her father's ex-girlfriends, Seraphina, and his best friend, Randy. Sarah described her father's activities as working, watching movies, spending time on the computer, dressing up for comic cons and zombie walks, and working on his car. She got good grades in school, but she didn't really have any friends her age and preferred to socialize with older people. Sarah had no idea about her father's troubled past with his mother, Ellen, and knew nothing about his violent behavior.

✑

Bryan's best friend, Randy, was interviewed twice by Marianne and William. Randy was an introvert, and it took a lot of pressing to get him to talk. Apparently, Randy and Bryan met at St. Vincent de Paul in the early 1990s and befriended each other. Randy would give Bryan rides to work. Randy worked in IT, and Bryan was a cook who later became a security guard. Bryan moved in with Randy in late 1992, after Angela's murder but before Melanie's. In addition to his IT work, Randy was an organist for several churches in the valley.

Bryan biked frequently, according to Randy, and would do so along the canal. Randy had found a blue turquoise suit in Bryan's stuff in his apartment around the time of Melanie's murder. He had found women's panties, which Bryan had apparently taken from his workplace. Randy had also noticed some oddities, such as a missing butcher knife as well as a bag that Bryan carried, which had mace in it. Randy passed along this information to some of the ladies at St. Vincent de Paul; this had generated the information that had been relayed to detectives and put in the packet on Bryan Miller. Randy was afraid to confront Bryan, as it was all suspicion and he had no proof. Randy later drafted a story of all these suspicions with the main character named Jack, which was a pseudonym for Bryan.

Randy could not bring himself to believe that Bryan brutally murdered Angela and Melanie. He told Marianne and William he had suspicions but didn't have any solid proof. Randy adamantly denied any involvement in the murders, and it appeared Bryan had some kind of bizarre control over him and likely used him for his money.

CHAPTER 24
THE GOOD NEWS AND LEARNING MORE

The key did not work. I knew it was the right one. I had used it a thousand times when I entered my house. Fatigue was the culprit, because I had been on a nonalcoholic bender. A celebration was in order, but that would have to wait. The arrest had set forth a chain of events, and I just needed a few hours of rest. Then I would get back at it.

Karyn opened the door. She must have heard me fumble with the keys. She pulled me close and we kissed.

She said, "I know you're exhausted, but I can't tell you how proud I am of you and your team. Congratulations, Sergeant Hillman! I knew you would do it!"

"I'm still in shock." My head throbbed, but I was proud. "Never give up, eh?"

"You guys never did!"

Karyn had been my cheerleader on the three-and-a-half-year hunt for the killer. She knew all about the CPA who chose an entirely different and unfamiliar path to try to make a difference. She learned about the war room I constructed to visualize the murders, the realization that I needed help, and how I built a talented team. Karyn followed us while we worked the clues, theorized on the military badass, chased down leads from the reports and files, researched other cases, and ventured to Philadelphia to meet Richard Walter and his Vidocq colleagues. She knew about the genealogist and groundbreaking DNA techniques. Every time a name was ruled out by DNA and I was discouraged, Karyn would remind me of the women and their families. She was an angel. The difference was now made, and it was the highlight of my career.

Karyn said, "It's all over the news. It even made the national news, babe!"

"That's awesome. I'm glad we gave those families some answers and some justice."

"Are their mothers okay?"

"Yes, we talked to them. They waited so long, but they were happy to hear the news."

I heard the baby cry. "I want to go see her."

I went into the nursery. I kissed my daughter on the forehead. "Your daddy is wiped out. I will tell you all about what my team did someday, little one."

I stumbled off and crawled in bed.

✍

"Dear boy, did you try to ring me on the telephone last night?" Richard asked.

"Yes, I wanted to just tell you that we arrested a guy on the canal murders you helped us with!"

"Oh, good, good, dear boy, that is delightful news! I told you he was in your files, didn't I? In the files, yes, yes, yes!"

"Yeah, you were spot on. We're totally excited, yet totally overwhelmed with the aftermath."

"Indeed, methinks that you would be. Many lesser-minded people think that it's all over with the arrest, but that's only the tip of the iceberg on such serial AEs. You have many things to look through and many people to talk to. Best of luck." He cackled.

Before he hung up, I told him in depth about the interview with Bryan. Bryan had toyed with us, just like Richard told us he would. Richard believed William did the best job he could. He, of course, would have brought the AE subtype to tears, just like the priest. I also told Richard about the interviews with Bryan's ex-wife, daughter, and best friend. Richard was not surprised that Bryan experimented with his ex-wife. In fact, he was not shocked by any of the information given.

"Did you find his lair?" Richard asked. "They all have one where they relive the murders and their fantasies."

We had not yet found Bryan's lair. If we didn't locate it in the house, then we would look for storage lockers. It would be massive for the investigation to find a lair that contained videotapes of the murders or scenes.

✑

My next call was to Colleen in California. She was very excited. She was already a rock star in the genealogy world, but this multidecade cold case positioned her as top forensic genealogist. Other agencies had used familial DNA searches like the California authorities did in the Grim Sleeper investigation. No other agency had used a forensic genealogist to help locate a serial killer of this magnitude. To my knowledge, we were the first in the fall of 2014.

I did remind her that our other savior, Richard, said he was in our files. Clark and I had worked the files from the extremes of the alphabet toward the middle. With 2,750 other cold cases mixed in, it might have taken us years, but eventually one of us would have stumbled on Bryan Miller lurking in the *M* section of the alphabet. Clark and I had too much experience to gloss over Bryan's file; it was an absolute bombshell. Nevertheless, Colleen had delivered the surname Miller to us, leading us to discover the file far faster than we would have otherwise. She had been instrumental in expediting our hunt to locate the killer.

✑

My mind spun. I looked at a file that had been handed to me by one of my detectives. It contained Bryan's juvenile court file, which we had not seen before. The file indicated he was of superior intelligence. *Just like Richard said*, I thought. *The Dahmer and Bundy subtypes always do. Crazy smart.* Bryan had an extensive history as a runaway with violent tendencies. The juvenile court leaders had gone so far as to propose a treatment plan. This treatment plan had been drafted approximately four months before he stabbed Celeste Bentley at Paradise Valley Mall. The plan detailed how Bryan managed his feelings with elaborate fantasy and escapism. The plan went on to describe him as angry, frustrated, depressed, emotionally immature, and destructive. *Destructive indeed. He has destroyed so many lives. If they only could have stopped him back then! And why didn't they? So many questions.*

I took a big sip of my coffee. I was exhausted, yet I wanted to know so much more about this monster. The plan indicated Bryan had a sexual behavior problem. A juvenile court judge even put in the file that he strongly recommended that Bryan be considered for the juvenile sex offenders program. Most of the rest of the records covered items that we already knew from file 668, like arson, shoplifting, and curfew.

I set the file aside, frustrated at the self-proclaimed Lucky Duck's luck and grabbed a DVD labeled "Time Capsule." I inserted it into my computer. I could see a very young and scrawny Bryan Miller along with other young people from the church. I stared. I still couldn't believe he was our theorized military badass. *No John Rambo there. DNA didn't lie, though, nor did his behavior file*, I thought. They were burying items in a time capsule as part of some project. It was from the summer of 1992, which was before our first canal murder. The group mentioned it would be dug up in twenty years. I think we all hoped for souvenirs or mention of the canal murders, but we found out later Bryan merely buried his St. Vincent de Paul identification card.

I grabbed a folder one of my detectives had put together labeled "Lucky Duck." I noticed a piece of paper showing Bryan's email address starting with "theduck13." There was a picture of a menacing cartoon duck holding a large knife, which was dripping with blood. This had been taken from Bryan's social media. I also noticed a DVD titled *The New York Ripper*. Bryan had this non-award-winning movie in his shopping cart online and had made reference to it. The detective purchased a copy for the squad to watch. In the meantime, I typed it into Google and watched the trailer. The sadistic killer went around brutally slashing women in New York City. He quacked like a duck when he killed them and also did so when he taunted police. My detectives had heard from friends and family that Bryan was known to inexplicably quack like a duck at various times. *Hollywood would love this guy*, I thought.

CHAPTER 25
THE HOUSE FROM HELL

S hocked was an understatement. I took a step backward and fell into a pile of old magazines and newspapers. A family of cockroaches scurried to an adjacent pile. I pushed myself up and stepped into a half-empty McDonald's carton containing crusted ketchup nestled against moldy fries. I cursed, but my full and undivided attention was locked on the full-sized shrink wrap over the refrigerator door. The shrink wrap art depicted the inside of a fridge with a woman's head in the freezer, hands and fingers on a shelf, and eyeballs in a jar. The original detective's theory held true. Without words, he just told us. This is, for the most part, what Bryan had done to Angela in 1992. I shuddered as I tried to comprehend it. Every time Bryan walked into his kitchen for the past twenty years, he ignited his fantasy of the kill and aftermath. *And he displayed it in plain sight*, I thought. Richard had tried to prepare me that these killers liked to play sarcastic ruses, but this was on a whole new level.

Bryan's house sat on the northwest corner of Mountain View and North 9th Street in North Central Phoenix. I studied a Google Maps aerial image of 844 East Mountain View Road. The map depicted an orderly, decent-sized mostly dirt lot (over 7,600 square feet). The lot bordered an alley to the north at the rear of the house, and a concrete pad for vehicles sat on the southeast side of the house, toward Ninth Street. I saw a large patio off the back of the house, and a small patio adorned the front. The house itself looked rather small at 1,053 square feet. *I'm not sure what they're complaining about with this search*, I thought.

I walked past the crime scene tape and toward the yard and immediately wadded up the map. It would be of no use in this bloated junkyard. A detective dressed in a protective suit offered me a suit, but I declined. I planned to merely show my support, get an update, and leave. I stepped over a rusty kid's bike and slid past a collection of opened Tidy Cats cat litter containers. However, my pant leg caught on a metal bookshelf and ripped. I cursed again. I needed to get to Clark and the house. The cat pee stench overwhelmed me to the point of nausea. I leaped over a large dusty ceiling fan and hurdled an engine block. "Damn it!" I yelled. My gray dress pants were now covered in grease.

Clark said, "Should have put on that special suit, boss."

"What in the hell have we gotten into?"

"I know. You ever seen anything like it?"

"Nope."

"Just wait until you see the inside."

I held my elbow to my nose but should have grabbed a gas mask. *Oh, and that protective suit. Bad call on that one*, I thought. The stench of cat urine outside shifted to an aroma of rotting food and mice feces. Swelled flies clung to the upper panes of the windows. I couldn't see the full view out of the window. Pile after pile of stuff blocked the windows to the four-foot-high mark. I couldn't tell what the floor covering was. *Was it carpet or tile?* I continued to forge deeper into the house, stepping on countless pizza boxes and newspapers. Cockroaches scampered with every step. I pushed against moving boxes and piles to keep my balance.

I eventually ran into Dom and JJ and saw the disheartened looks in their eyes. Even the normally bubbling Dom seemed dismayed, and he didn't have a witty anecdote. I had no good words of encouragement and felt bad for them, but I knew that we had to do this part. We had to plow through this serial killer's belongings and try to locate the tools of his trade and the treasures he took from his victims along the way. However, the conditions of this house from hell had, for the most part, stomped out our hopes of finding a great piece of evidence.

Clark showed me their keenly devised plan to tackle this cluster of a search warrant. Clark pointed to the schematic, depicting how they had divided the property into sectors A through J. The team had acquired two massive steel moving pods from a local vendor as well as at least a hundred large plastic storage bins from Home Depot to use as sorting bins. The pods would be used as temporary securable storage lockers to be later transported to our crime laboratory. A centralized station in the rear yard was created to sort, number, photograph, and package evidence. I could see the large team of investigators already using the centralized station.

Admittedly, I was glad to leave the horrid house. I couldn't believe that anyone could live there and was appalled that Bryan made his teenage daughter endure those conditions. I needed to organize the team who would handle incoming tips from citizens and law enforcement agencies on other crimes. We would also coordinate the local and out-of-state interviews to be conducted and ensure the county attorney's team had what they needed to begin the adjudication phase. Oh, and I also needed to change my filthy clothes.

☙

Impressively, in less than a week, the dog-tired search warrant team had wrapped up their deep-dive search at the house from hell and had seized more than six thousand pieces of evidence, which were itemized, photographed, and sorted into more than 761 packages. Unfortunately, Clark and a few team members would spend another two weeks entering the items into the property management system.

Over two decades had passed since our murders. It was a long shot, but we searched for items taken from Angela's and Melanie's scenes. The bikes, the Walkmans, and the knife were at the top of the list. We also hoped to locate evidence from other unknown victims. This wasn't the case. As with the refrigerator shrink wrap, we found items that painted a more complete picture of the monster we now knew, Bryan Miller.

A sample of items seized included:

- Women's necklaces and jewelry boxes with women's jewelry.
- A holster marked "deputy," which was possibly his mom's.
- His mother's diary from May 24, 1982, to May 18, 1983. One had an entry on March 17, 1983, saying she found an X-rated book in Bryan's backpack.
- A US Secret Service jacket with some type of staining on it.
- A plastic doll of a woman inside a box labeled the "Visible Woman." A person could in effect dissect the parts from the doll. Within the box, there were a heart, a liver, and intestines made of molded plastic.
- A Post-it Note with a drawing. The drawing, titled "Murder Scene," depicted a person standing with a large head wound.
- A picture of an unknown blond girl in a cheerleading outfit.
- Photos of women in swimsuits with bottoms on but no tops.
- A newspaper article that described unsolved murders in the late 1980s in the Phoenix metropolitan area.
- An article titled "On Finding a Model," which described

how an artist wanting a nude body model recruits, with a model release form attached.

- A discipline referral form from when Bryan was in seventh grade. The teacher wrote, "Bryan screamed at other students and at me in class today. He also used profanity by calling the students assholes. He was really having a problem today!"
- A school bus incident to parents written by a bus driver that says, "pushed his way through me and a teacher after we tried to question his involvement in another incident on the bus. Bryan was screaming at me while I was trying to talk to him."
- Photograph of a zombie creature cutting off a breast of a woman.
- Three developed human teeth in a jar.
- A book about Jack the Ripper.
- Multiple Barbie dolls (all missing their feet).
- A large number of violent porn videos depicting torture and bondage of women: One had a woman tied to a large stick impaled as if she were a pig ready for a roast, others showed women with body parts cut off and lots of blood.
- Rope, gloves, binoculars, and other tools suitable for hunting.
- Numerous references to the 1982 slasher movie *The New York Ripper*.

❧

I walked over to the crime lab and saw the now infamous Zombie Hunter car parked in an examination bay. The car had been well taken care of by Bryan. It was his baby and his fantasy. I asked the crime scene specialist if she had found anything. She said she had processed it with luminol, a blood enhancement reagent, but nothing reacted. She took a pair of handcuffs, brass knuckles, a white towel with what appeared to be fake bloodstains, XL gloves, and a zombie mannequin from the trunk.

All props for his elaborate zombie hunter fantasy, I thought.

〜

Clark and I met with the lab to go over the items seized from Bryan's house. Clark had carefully selected items he believed might have our victims' or other victims' DNA.

"Kelley, I've listed out a decent number of items that I would like tested from Bryan's house," said Clark. He slid his paperwork to her.

"Okay, let's go through them," she said. "I think we're good to look at all the saw blades, the knives, sheaths, hatchet, Sony cassette recorder, Sony headphones, wad of brown hair, brown electrical cord with brown hair, rusty chain, and electrical wire with hairs attached. I think we can look at the three teeth you found, but I need to double check."

"Sounds good. Thank you! Hopefully, we can find something."

Unfortunately, these items did not yield any trace of our victims' DNA or that of any unidentified victim.

We had to be thorough. This whole investigation would be picked apart in the years to come.

CHAPTER 26
THE OTHERS

I sat in my home office while Karyn and the baby were asleep. I needed sleep, but my mind churned and wouldn't stop. The FBI profile read, "Fantasies become more elaborate after both murders—killer would not stop." *Who else? Who else did you kill, Bryan?* We needed to find out.

Mark prepared a timeline. I pulled it out of my backpack and studied it. I wanted to decode it. I circled Angela and Melanie in 1992 and 1993, respectively. I located the 1989 assault at Paradise Valley Mall. I wrote in my notepad "starting point?"

I followed the entries and took notes.

- 5/26/92—Brandy Myers disappeared. Young girl who matched information given by Bryan's ex-wife. I wrote, "Missing Persons Detective Stu to handle investigation and present to Maricopa County Attorney's Office. I think Miller is definitely good for it. Difficult to prove, unfortunately, due to time, no evidence, and no body. Nobody homicides are always the most difficult—Get further details and update from Stu on this case. It's in great hands with Stu."
- 5/28/92—Shannon Aumock murdered. Decomposed body found under a piece of plywood between the dirt roadway and the Central Arizona Project Canal at 2000

E. Deer Valley Road. Anonymous caller reported seeing a body while riding an ATV in the desert area. Detectives stated it would not have been possible to see the body. The call seemed rather suspect. This call originated at the same time as people were looking for Brandy Myers, as it was highly publicized. It looked like the caller was later revealed and had a warrant, which was the reason for his deceptiveness. I wrote, "Shannon kind of looks like Brandy with glasses. Unable to tell whether Shannon was stabbed in the back like Angela and Melanie. Lab tests for all her clothing and other items negative for DNA. Tough case."

- 10/23/92—Diana Vicari, dismembered in Tucson, AZ. Murder month before Angela's murder. Nothing like it in Tucson since. I wrote, "Tucson PD at a dead end. No DNA. Diana was at a concert before her murder. Maybe Bryan traveled to Tucson to attend and killed her afterwards? Distinct possibility."

- 4/17/93—Valerie Brown attacked by an unknown suspect with a club; she was jogging along the canal around 3200 E Stanford. After Bryan was arrested, she called in, said that Bryan was her attacker. I wrote, "Discuss with attorneys. Problem—so much publicity of Bryan's arrest. Not sure if have enough to charge with no evidence and significant time frame."

- 1995—Bryan married Amy. I wrote, "Dormant with no kills? Richard said this could happen with AEs. Or was Amy just a cover?"

- July 1999—His daughter, Sarah, born.

- 1999–2003—Bryan lived in the State of Washington. I wrote, "What did he do there besides the acts below?"

- 10/5/99—Bryan filed a stolen bicycle report with Everett

Police Department. I wrote, "sarcastic ruse?"

- 10/9/00—Victoria Mikelsen was assaulted in a knife attack near Interurban Trail in Everett, Washington. Report purged. I wrote, "William and Marianne to interview. Bryan lived very close to the scene. Can Washington authorities move it forward now? It's out of Phoenix Police jurisdiction."

- 5/23/02—Bryan arrested for stabbing of Melissa Ruiz-Ramirez in Everett, Washington.

- 5/24/02 to 12/19/02—Bryan incarcerated in Snohomish County correctional facility. He was acquitted at trial for the stabbing, as his attorney convinced the jury that Ruiz-Ramirez was a known prostitute. Ruiz-Ramirez died of an overdose in 2007. I wrote, "Adjudicated with not guilty. She's deceased. Nothing we can do. Bryan got away with it."

- 2003—Traffic citations in Washington. I wrote, "nothing violent noted. Just not caught for it?"

- October and December 2003—returned to AZ. I wrote, "significant gap. Who else?"

- January 2006—Filed for divorce from Amy; finalized on 2/13/07.

- 12/18/10—His mother, Martha "Ellen" Miller, died of natural causes.

- 2011–2014—Several traffic tickets but no other arrests.

- 2013—Teenager Adrienne Salinas partial remains found in Apache Junction. She had been abducted in Tempe. I wrote, "Tempe PD to handle. We passed along information on Bryan. It's their case. I don't think they ever found her head. Might be tough to prove?"

- January 2015—Arrested for murders of Angela and Melanie. I wrote, "the Lucky Duck's luck finally ran out!"

I looked down at the summary of the FBI profile. *Now that we know what we know about Bryan, how close were they?* I marked yes or no on the list for each major point. Some were a given.

- Almost identical stab wound to Angela—YES
- In both cases, all cutting and activities done after death— YES
- Re-dressing Melanie into bathing suit—violent sexual fantasy—YES
- Killer spent a lot of time at crime scene—YES
- Angela and Melanie were victims of opportunity—YES
- Approach of stabbing them on bike part of fantasy— blitz-style attack—YES
- Divergence of behavior between murders—eroticized fantasy—YES
- Killer largely disorganized, but bringing suit to scene showed some organization—YES
- Killer impulsive with intense desire to fulfill fantasy given these populated areas—YES
- Fantasies become more elaborate after both murders— killer would not stop—YES
- Killer may be mental health patient under care and strong possibility hospitalized or incarcerated after Melanie's murder due to inactivity since 1993—NO
- Killer has collection of violent porn with detective-style magazines—YES

The FBI was right on most of it, except for the hospitalization or incarceration. He wasn't dead, either, as public opinion believed. I doodled on my notepad. I hoped the act would give me some shred of a clue, because I needed to link him to other crimes. I gave Bryan what the golf world calls a mulligan for the botched assault at Paradise Valley Mall. He was terrible at his craft—it was broad daylight; there were witnesses; he hid near the scene, confessed, and even drew the knife for detectives. I wondered how he could be so precise with Angela and Melanie just a few years after Paradise Valley Mall. He took his time with our murders. He mostly avoided detection, other than possibly by the witnesses listed in the supplements who saw a man carrying an object and a man near the church. I wrote, "did he have help?"

Brandy Myers was a defenseless child. He took advantage of that situation on his own turf inside his apartment. I had no idea on Shannon Aumock. She was a runaway teenager. There wasn't enough to go on. I wrote, "law enforcement records only so good for the timeline—lots of gaps." I pushed my notepad away in frustration. *There had to be more. Maybe in Washington?*

When Marianne, William, and the two solid detectives from Missing Persons, Stu Somershoe and Melissa Pulver (formerly Lutch) got back from Washington, we debriefed in the conference room. They discovered that a lot of Washington law enforcement agencies purge their reports after a period. In stark contrast, Arizona agencies seem to archive everything. A lot of useful details can be found in old reports—especially on serial killers.

Despite the roadblocks, the team was able to piece things together with court documents and by speaking with the victims there. Bryan assaulted a woman named Melissa Marie Ruiz-Ramirez on May 23, 2002, in Everett, Washington. Apparently, she said that she needed to use the phone, and Bryan offered to give her a ride to a canopy shop. Bryan worked at the canopy shop, and Ruiz-Ramirez went with him because he looked familiar. When they got there, no one was there. She went to use the phone, and as she was looking down at it to dial, Bryan came up from behind, grabbed her with his left arm around the chest, and stabbed her in the back. Ruiz-Ramirez fought back and was stabbed three more times before she could grab the knife. In doing so, she cut her hand. For reasons unknown, Bryan let her get away, and she called the police. Bryan was arrested a few blocks away.

Was he rusty? Did he not plan? Marianne and William believed Bryan just acted and didn't think it through. Richard's "pathology trumps intellect" applied here. Bryan's pathology to kill overrode his knowledge of the risks.

Bryan apparently hired a good attorney, who was able to paint Ruiz-Ramirez as a strung-out and non-credible prostitute to the jury. Since it was her word against his, and they couldn't bring into evidence his Paradise Valley Mall knife attack when he was a juvenile, he was found not guilty. The Snohomish County sheriff's detective who helped them out said the victim, Ruiz-Ramirez, died in 2007 of a drug overdose.

Marianne and William did find another incident that Bryan was most likely good for back then. They had to piece it together, as the department had purged a lot of it. On October 9, 2000, Everett PD took a report of an assault with a knife. The girl was on what they call the Interurban Trail when she was attacked and stabbed. Bryan lived in an apartment close to that trail.

They spoke to the girl who was attacked, Victoria Mikelson. She told them that early one morning, she was walking when a man came up and stabbed her in the back and suddenly was on top of her. She said she fought back and at one point got the knife, and the man ran away. She had been stabbed over twenty times. It was a miracle she survived the attack. The description she gave closely matched Bryan. Unfortunately, there was no chance to charge Bryan with this attack. The report and evidence were largely destroyed.

Bryan's family in Washington wouldn't speak with the detectives. His family members couldn't believe that Bryan was connected to our murders or any others, for that matter. The detectives talked to several coworkers and his supervisor in Washington. They all said that Bryan was reliable and a good worker at the canopy company; however, he was quiet, disheveled, and kept to himself.

❧

I shut the door to my office. I needed time away from the chaos. Trying to keep tabs and stay up to speed on all of the tasks of the team members during the arrest aftermath had taken a definite toll on me. Yet, I wanted to learn more about Bryan, and we all wanted to ensure successful prosecution for the canal murders and accountability for *all* of his misdeeds. I picked up the file on Brandy Myers. The canal murders investigation was in the hands of the prosecutors at this point, and one never wants to call it a victory until successful prosecution is attained. We all collectively felt we had him dead to rights on our two canal murders. However, we knew Bryan was good for many more murders. You don't start off cutting off a victim's head and leave off re-dressing a young woman after a postmortem sexual assault. There had to be victims before and after these crimes. Sadly, we just couldn't find the victims or prove his guilt in the attacks and murders we thought he did. The Brandy Myers case was the closest and would be the nail in the coffin, so to speak, for Bryan Patrick Miller.

Stu, a top-notch detective from Missing Persons with a ton of intelligence, passion, and attention to detail, had the Brandy Myers case. I knew it was in great hands. If anyone could deliver Brandy and her family justice, it would be Stu. He was like a prized bloodhound.

I delved into the details of the file. Brandy was thirteen years old at the time she disappeared in May 1992, but investigators noted she was slower in cognitive and emotional development than her peers. I peered at her school photo in the file. I sighed with sadness. She was a beautiful young girl with straight blond hair and blue eyes. She wore eyeglasses and had an infectious smile. According to notes in the file, she was very close to her sister, Kristin.

Kristin was two years younger than Brandy but looked out for her. Brandy was sometimes bullied. Kristin wouldn't stand for it. Brandy and Kristin lived with their mother and stepfather in the Sunnyslope area. Their neighborhood was a high-crime and lower-income area with a saturation of drug activity. Brandy was in sixth grade at Sunnyslope Elementary School and walked with her sister to and from school. They always took the same route.

On May 26, 1992, Brandy had asked Kristin to go around the neighborhood with her and collect money for books. (It should be noted Bryan had told his ex-wife, Amy, that the girl he pulled into his apartment and killed in 1992 before the canal murders was collecting money for what he claimed and/or Amy misunderstood was Girl Scout cookies and not for books. Regardless of this inconsistency, all of the other circumstantial evidence in the case later pointed to Bryan.) Kristin was busy with friends and declined, so Brandy walked the neighborhood alone.

Brandy never returned home, and her family called the police. Officers circulated in the area, but Stu noted that their focus seemed to be more on a missing child than on a child abduction. There was no organized door-to-door canvass, and the documentation was sketchy at best. Stu had gone on a mission to fill in the gaps. I noted that someone had called in to say they saw Brandy at a nearby grocery store that evening. The information was inexplicably never substantiated and allegedly came from a child. Unfortunately, it appeared to be a distraction and dead end. The media coverage was intense during the immediate aftermath, and hundreds of concerned citizens arrived in the area to help police search for Brandy. Investigators quickly ruled out any foul play by her mother, stepfather, or biological father. Leads surfaced over the following years and were looked at, but the lack of physical evidence and the fact that her body was never found led to the difficult cold case being shelved.

The case had just been resurrected when Bryan Patrick Miller confessed to his ex-wife that he had pulled a "Girl Scout" inside his apartment, put her in a bathtub, cut her up, and later discarded her in his trash. Stu was able to show that Bryan's apartment at the time was yards away from Brandy's house, not to mention she had last been seen by neighbors going door to door very close to his apartment. It all lined up.

Stu and his team executed a search warrant on Bryan's old apartment in February 2015, just a month after we arrested Bryan for the canal murders. Over twenty years had passed, but it was worth a shot. Stu found dried blood evidence near the bathtub, but it unfortunately did not match Brandy's DNA.

I finally set the file down and rubbed my eyes. I felt a wave of sadness for Brandy and her family. Her sister, Kristin, had been through hell, beating herself up for not going with Brandy that evening. *How was she to know, though? Kristin was just a child, too.* Brandy had unknowingly met the monster we now knew as Bryan Patrick Miller.

❧

Stu and I eventually interviewed Bryan for his role in the Brandy Myers case. The interview went on for well over two hours before Bryan requested an attorney. The self-proclaimed Zombie Hunter merely toyed with us, as Richard the profiler said he would do. The case was later submitted to the county attorney, but it was turned down due to no reasonable likelihood of conviction. This meant the prosecutors believed there wasn't enough evidence to prove Bryan did it beyond the circumstantial proximity of his apartment and his statements to his wife. Stu, the family, and I were understandably upset at this decision.

❧

After the arrest, for the better part of a year, my dedicated team, along with Stu and Melissa from Missing Persons, worked thousands of hours and interviewed countless people who had interacted with Bryan since his adolescent years. We broke them into groups based on time period: his juvenile detention days in Adobe Mountain, the days when he lived and worked at an at-risk youth group called Aim Right Ministries, his time with the Mennonite church, his days at St. Vincent de Paul, his steampunk association group, his comic con dress-up adventures, his zombie-hunting days, his renaissance festival associates, and his stepfathers. The consensus seemed to be that Bryan was a shy loner type who was unkempt and had poor hygiene and body odor. Most were in disbelief that the man they knew as the Lucky Duck was capable of such raw violence.

He hid in plain sight in front of these folks for decades. Steampunk, comic con, zombie hunting, and renaissance festivals were all fantasies for this master of deception.

CHAPTER 27

THE LAIR AND THE BAD BEHAVIOR

T he hidden room was rather small and dimly lit, sequestered from natural light. The air was stale from lack of circulation. Yellowed newspaper articles blanketed the room. The articles collectively spoke of murder. Drawings of female desecration and destruction supported the theme of the articles. Despite the deviancy, the artist admittedly was talented, almost at a professional level. Stacks upon stacks of Polaroid pictures were scattered throughout, and hand-labeled videotapes sat on the bookshelf. A collection of old Walkmans were nestled together in a large shoebox. I aimed my flashlight and read the label on the video: "Angela 1992." The next read "Melanie 1993." *This is it! Hot dog! This is the lair we have been looking for!*

Karyn shook my shoulder and said, "Troy, wake up! You're having a bad dream."

"What? Huh?" I said. Groggy and struggling to separate reality from fiction, I said, "Crap! I had a dream we found Bryan's lair."

"You'll find it. I have faith in you and your team, just like I did with you solving the murders."

"I hope so," I said.

Along with the spot-on insight that "he's in your files" and "pathology trumps intellect every time," Richard told us repeatedly these AE subtypes *always* keep lairs. He referenced the likes of Ted Bundy, Jeffrey Dahmer, and John Wayne Gacy. They would use basements, crawl spaces, cellars, sheds, barns, and even storage lockers. It was their secret and sacred place, a place where they would typically masturbate and relive the fantasy over and over. In this lair, they would keep Polaroids and other pictures, videotapes, trophies and souvenirs from the victim, newspaper clippings, and favorite weapons. It was statistically likely that Bryan would do the same.

We all knew that locating this lair would be damning for Bryan at trial. Not only would it potentially add evidence to the case for the murders of Angela and Melanie, but it would fill in large gaps for us before, between, and after the murders. Despite the absolute mess of it, Bryan's house had been searched inside and out for weeks. Bomb squad detectives had even x-rayed the walls and found nothing—no secret rooms or stash areas. The house sat on a concrete pad, so there were no secret crawl spaces in the floors—this was verified by the US Border Patrol, who used a ground-penetrating radar contraption that looked like an Igloo cooler on wheels with a pull rope on the outside of the house. The radar looked for disruptions in the soil that could indicate digging or buried items. They, too, found nothing at the current house, and they took it a step further: They searched all of Bryan's known addresses from the past for disturbances and buried items. Nothing was found.

∽

I assigned Dom and JJ to the task of finding the lair, asking them to concentrate on storage lockers in Phoenix. Sources close to Bryan told us he liked storage lockers and had rented them through the years.

"What about the storage lockers? We still haven't found his lair. Richard tells me that they *all* have a lair. Why can't you find it, Dominator?" I asked.

"The Dominator can only dominate so much!" said Dom.

"We sent a flyer out to all the storage lockers in the valley," JJ said. "We've had numerous calls and checked them all out. Apparently, Bryan cleaned out a locker in December, before we made the arrest. Who knows what was in that, but Bryan told the manager that he ran out of money to pay for it."

"I want that lair, Kid and Dom!" I said.

"Maybe we will have to settle for what we found in that house from hell," said JJ. "He couldn't afford anything else. That took years off my life, by the way."

"You remember that fantasy letter that his mother found while he was in juvenile corrections?" I asked.

"Yeah," said Dom.

"You remember that he wrote 'videotape' in his wicked plan? That tells me he was thinking about it then and possibly videotaped his attacks on Angela and Melanie," I said.

❧

The search for the lair went on for months and then years. Dom and JJ worked diligently on it. Sadly, we never found it. If a lair does exist, hopefully it will be discovered by a third party and reported to police, or Bryan will divulge it at some point before he dies.

❧

Marianne and William darted into my office. Marianne said, "The forensic guys up at ACTIC are done with Bryan's hard drives that they could open and the phones. They want us to come up to their facility and view them. Do you want to come?"

"Good Lord! You scared me!"

The three of us took a jaunt up north to the Arizona Counter Terrorism Information Center's remote and secure facility. We were escorted back to a warehouse-type room with rows and rows of pristine tables blanketed with a mass of computers with even more monitors. We gathered around as the forensic investigator walked us through the different files. Bryan had stored thousands of images.

"As you can see, he definitely had a thing for topless women," said the forensic detective. "You will see that there are a ton of rather violent pornographic images. Lots of women getting stabbed, cut open, beheaded, limbs removed, tortured, strangled, cooked . . . Um, basically, an extensive collage of the overall and complete desecration of females. You name it with women, he was into it. He even had one folder named 'Bryans Favs,' which had all of the above, including autopsy photos."

"I just don't understand how someone could get turned on by this stuff," said Marianne.

The forensic investigator said, "So, there were a couple of homemade-type videos in here. Nothing related to your murders, murders of women, or depicting Bryan, but people getting killed in rather bizarre scenes. We don't think that they are real, but we can't say with one hundred percent certainty."

"Any kiddie porn?" asked Marianne.

"Yeah, there's some. We are working with a detective from internet crimes against children. She has an expert who can opine on ages for the courts."

We requested a host of charges for the child pornography against Bryan. We were later told it was dismissed due to a technicality on how the warrant was written. We were upset, to say the least. *Hopefully, the Lucky Duck couldn't beat the charges we had on him from Angela and Melanie. Time would tell that, too.*

❧

A detective gathered a small group of us in the conference room to go over his findings from reviewing all the DVD and VHS tapes found in Bryan's house. We prayed Bryan had recorded our murders. This would answer so many more questions. He had left the how on the table during his interview. Yet, there were no spliced tapes and nothing related to our murders or any others. However, the detective found tons of disturbing violent pornography. The names were chilling, especially in light of what we knew about Bryan: *Dr. Jekyll and Mistress Hyde*, *Ninja Assassins*, *Just Over 18*, *Wanted Teen Offenders*, *True Blood, Season 1*, *Blood Relic*, *Buried Alive*, *Murder Party*, *Stay Alive*, *Blood and Sex Nightmare*, *Blood Fest-All You Can Eat*, *Amateur Porn Star Killer 2*, and *An Erotic Vampire in Paris 3*. All had graphic violence, and some had decapitation scenes. I felt sorry for the detective who had to pore through them. I remember thinking, *He might need therapy.*

✌

Marianne pushed a picture in front of me. I recognized it as the artwork following the "Tweety!" inscription on the tunnel walls from Melanie's murder in 1993. It was the cartoon character of a man in a fedora.

"Yeah, the man in the fedora?" I said. I wondered where she was going with this.

Marianne said, "Boss, William and I found something more to it."

"What do you mean?"

"So, Bryan was nicknamed the duck, and he was quite proud of it, using it on social media accounts, right? So, we got to looking at the fedora man. Look at it again, boss, and carefully look for a duck."

"Okay."

"You see it, boss?" she asked. "Here's the bill of the duck and his eyes." She traced it for me.

"Aw, it's a damn image within an image. The mind wants to see a man in a fedora, but if told, it sees the duck also. That's brilliant! On both his part and yours for seeing that!"

"Yup, a duck!" said Marianne.

"Not a Lucky Duck, though. Any further progress on the Tweety or the WSC carvings and art?"

"Methinks not," said William.

"Well, in your spare time not getting this thing ready for trial, figure it out."

I sat there and stared out my office window. The good Lord may not have given Bryan a badass military body like we had presumed, but he did give Bryan a supreme talent. Bryan was a badass with his pencil and paper. He could draw detailed pictures that Walt Disney himself would be proud of. In fact, I'm not sure why he didn't use this prolific talent in some type of graphic arts or design career. *If so, maybe the fates would have led things to turn out differently. Maybe Angela, Melanie, and Brandy would still be alive.*

CHAPTER 28
THE EX-GIRLFRIENDS

I pulled into the coffee shop nestled in a strip mall in South Scottsdale. I lived in a home on the east side of Phoenix designated as the Arcadia district, so this wasn't a far drive at all. I needed to get away from the buzzing beehive of headquarters and its unceasing tractor beam that wanted to pull me into time-sucking meetings led by management. I needed to get away from the madness and just process and assess. Many believed the arrest was the end of this massive investigation, but it was not. There was so much to do and learn, especially in a capital murder case involving a serial killer, like this one.

The coffee shop wasn't trendy, like the double-soy-latte places that were popping up all around the Valley of the Sun with their bizarre loud music and oblivious customers screaming into their cellphones. Rather, it was quaint and relaxing. It was a hidden gem for cops wanting to get away from the chaos of their shifts. The soothing aroma of coffee hit one's nostrils immediately upon breaching the front wooden door. The shop was built on simplicity—another thing most cops liked. There were only three drinks on the menu, and they came in the standard sizes of small, medium, and large: regular, espresso, and Americano. The floors were painted concrete; the ceilings had completely exposed wiring, pipes, and vents; and the unfinished walls had only a few desert landscape paintings from local artists. I found a booth in a corner.

It was time for me to learn more about Bryan Patrick Miller. Every good detective is well acquainted with the saying "Hell hath no fury like a woman scorned." In many investigations, the ex-wives and ex-girlfriends are typically a gold mine of telling information on a suspect. Bryan's ex-wife, Amy, had delivered a bombshell about his deviant acts in their sex life and his confession of murdering and chopping up a young girl when he was living in an apartment hosted by the Mennonite church.

I took a big drink from my simple black coffee and plugged my headphones into my laptop. I grabbed my steno pad and wrote "Ex-Girlfriends" across the top. I hit the Play button on the file labeled "Tura." Tura had been interviewed recently by Stu and Melissa; they were now a part of the Miller investigation thanks to Brandy originally being in their cold case missing persons work. Stu and Melissa were a blessing and a massive addition to the already elite team.

Tura told detectives she had met Bryan in February or March 2012. She met him at a local steampunk group dinner. They began dating in May 2012, and it lasted for about five months. She lived with Bryan at his house on Mountain View, where the search warrant had recently been served. Tura said the house had been packed with stuff and described a hoarding situation. Bryan had told her he inherited many things from his mother, which included a large collection of hair barrettes and hair accessories. I wrote in my notepad: "Did he collect these from victims too?"

According to Tura, Bryan also liked to collect things like movies, posters, memorabilia, figurines, dolls, video games, and art. His favorite movies were of zombies, and he had a fascination with actresses Anne Hathaway and Marilyn Monroe. He enjoyed shows like *Buffy the Vampire Slayer*, *Dr. Who*, and *Star Trek*. Bryan preferred heavy metal music, but he would listen to other genres. I wrote in my notepad, "Girl murdered in Tucson in 1992 was killed at heavy metal concert I believe—follow up."

Tura described Bryan as extremely shy, quiet, very reserved, and not very communicative about his personal life or history. She went on to say he was secretive about his past and added it was too difficult to talk about. Bryan had told Tura about his arrest in Washington. He told her it was a self-defense situation when the woman tried to rob him. Bryan never told her about his juvenile arrest for stabbing the woman at Paradise Valley Mall. I wrote in my notepad: "Manipulative." He did say that he was in a juvenile jail but blamed it on his mother. He told Tura his mother put him there because they fought nonstop.

Tura described what she knew of Bryan's background. He was born in either Michigan or Minnesota and moved to Hawaii at a very young age. His father was in the military and killed in a motorcycle accident. Bryan and his mother relocated to Glendale, a suburb of Phoenix, to live with Bryan's grandmother. Tura said Bryan's relationship with his mother was tumultuous. Bryan described his mother to Tura as overbearing and over-protective. Because of his mother, Bryan had few friends. Bryan blamed his mother for his inability to have relationships with women and added his mother was emotionally and physically abusive to him. Despite the abuse, Bryan told her he was with his mother when she died in Washington. He would cry when he discussed his mother.

Bryan had described to Tura a member of the Paradise Valley Mennonite Church who had helped him with a room when he got out of juvenile prison. He had rented his current home and prior apartment in the Sunnyslope area of Phoenix from a woman named Agnes. Tura said Bryan's closest friend was Randy. They seemed almost like brothers to her, and Randy seemed sort of like a mentor to Bryan. Randy told her after the arrest that he and Bryan lived together during the time of the second canal murder. Randy told her that the evidence was very strong, but he didn't want to believe Bryan did it. However, he couldn't deny the facts. Bryan would always ride his bikes in the same area as the crime scenes.

Tura described Bryan as very controlling. He had very firm rules about cooking and access to areas of the house. When she broke a rule, Bryan would respond with what she called the silent treatment and sulk. She never saw Bryan exhibit violent behavior, but he admitted to her that when he was younger, he would get rages and engage in violence. He added that he would black out and not remember what happened during these so-called rages. Tura said she felt like she was on pins and needles and finally moved out. She felt bad for Bryan, as he had apparently been rejected a lot. I wrote in my notepad: "Planting his defense of rages and blackouts years before the arrest?"

My coffee was empty. I asked for a refill and plowed on. Tura painted a picture of Bryan's character. There was no scorn, just pure honesty. Some of it reinforced what we already knew, but the rest built out the monster we had hunted for three and a half years.

According to Tura, Bryan could have suffered from bipolar disorder due to excessive highs and lows. He refused treatment and told her that the psychologist during his divorce gave him medication, which made him excessively tired. Tura said Bryan valued two things the most: his daughter and his car. Tura added, though, that she believed Bryan put his needs before Sarah's. His daughter was then forced to in effect mimic his interests.

Tura described Bryan's sex drive as really low and said they had sex only a few times over the months they lived together. He preferred anal sex, but there were no fetishes or violence in their sex life. Tura added that Bryan was obsessed by ducks and considered the number 13 to be his lucky number. Bryan loved to draw and sketched pin-ups of girls. He was also in a filmmaking group. I wrote down "obsession with ducks, artist, and filmmaking."

I got up and stretched. I triaged my text messages and phone calls. Nothing uber important. More coffee followed. We had found four ex-girlfriends, and I had one more interview to go through at the coffee shop. Marianne and William promised to give me a summary of the other two later that afternoon.

I found the file labeled "Heather" and hit Play. Heather told detectives she met Bryan through a mutual friend at a party in October 2013. They began dating a few weeks later, but the relationship lasted only about a month. She did not live with Bryan and never visited his hoarder house on Mountain View. She described Bryan as a quiet and decent guy. He was into nerdy things like steampunk and comic con. He liked zombie and horror movies. Also, he liked Japanese anime culture.

She never saw Bryan become violent and believed he was a good parent to his daughter, Sarah. She did not see any evidence of drug or alcohol abuse or physical or psychological issues. Heather said Bryan had the ability to study something he was interested in intensely and develop great knowledge on it.

When asked about their sex life, she told them they had sex only once. It was what she described as normal vaginal intercourse. There was no bondage, fetishes, or deviant behavior.

Bryan had told Heather about an arrest for arson as a juvenile but gave no details. Bryan did not tell her about any other arrests in his past. He did not talk about his parents, but he did talk about his ex-wife. He called her crazy and said she used drugs. Heather added that their circle of friends used a website called DeviantArt. I wrote down in my notepad: "DeviantArt."

The audio file ended. I packed up my things and left the cozy confines of the coffee shop to head into the bustling headquarters.

❧

I pulled the door open, entered, and saw Marianne and William seated in a quiet conference room away from the madness of our work area. I had asked the two hard chargers to take a break from their post-arrest interviews and get me up to speed on the other two girlfriends, Seraphina and Marilyn.

"Hi, boss," Marianne said. She was always chipper. However, both of them looked exhausted. It had been a nonstop journey since the day of Bryan's arrest.

"After all this is over, I'm gonna order you two to take a long vacation," I said. The two were not known to want to take any vacation. They wanted to be solving murders for their victims and families.

"It's what we signed up for," William said.

"So, tell me about Seraphina," I said.

Marianne began, "It was a really long interview, but she told us some interesting things. She was the first girlfriend after his ex-wife, Amy. This was all pre-Tura, Heather, and Marilyn. Seraphina dated him from early 2006 to the middle of 2008. They worked at the Arizona Renaissance Festival together, which is where they met. Bryan seemed nervous and awkward to her at first. He told her about his daughter, Sarah, and said he was divorcing Amy. He told her his wife had left him. Seraphina didn't want to date him until he was officially divorced, so they started in the summer of 2006."

"I can't say that I blame Amy for leaving the man," I said. "The man stuck pins in her private parts!"

William smirked and said, "Seraphina said Bryan was really into cars and bikes. In the beginning, he was nice, polite, and romantic. Seraphina said Bryan told her several times that his wife left him. He told her that his wife cheated on him and his heart was broken. He wanted to fix the marriage, but she walked out on him."

"Playing the victim again," I said. "He's quite good at that."

Marianne said, "Seraphina felt bad for him. The divorce made him anxious and depressed. Bryan wanted to live together and marry, but she wasn't sure. She moved in with him anyway in late 2006."

"Into the house from hell? The one we searched on Mountain View?" I said.

"Yup. She said it was cluttered with stacked boxes but not as bad back then," William said.

Marianne said, "Seraphina really cared about his daughter, Sarah. They had a very good relationship, but it caused issues. Bryan seemed to want Seraphina's undivided attention. He wanted to be with her all the time, and he got upset when she left. She said she felt stuck in the middle between Bryan and Sarah, with both wanting her. If she didn't give Bryan attention, he would storm off and sulk. He was never violent with her or his daughter. Seraphina did say, though, that he had a bad temper and would get angry easily. He would throw things and punch walls. He would then mainly pout and cry."

"What was their sex life like?" I asked.

"Seraphina said she didn't want to have sex until she was married. This caused a ton of fights and was a core problem in their relationship. She said they never had sex but did fool around and do other things, though," Marianne said.

"Did Bryan show any deviant behavior during these fooling around times?" I asked.

"He would sometimes grab her by the neck and squeeze. Seraphina said it was more passionate and not really aggressive, though. She would just move his hand away."

"Interesting," I said. "Richard would love that little nugget."

William said, "Get this. Bryan told Seraphina that his ex-wife was really into choking and liked kinky, wild, violent sex things."

"Wait. He blamed the ex-wife? He was the one who cut her hair during sex and poked her with needles, right?"

Marianne and William both nodded.

"What did she say Bryan told her about his past?" I said.

Marianne said, "Bryan told her he was born in Michigan. When he was very little, the family moved to Hawaii. He said his dad was in the Army and died in an accident in Hawaii. His mother beat him up and abused him. Bryan told Seraphina that he blacked out when he realized he stabbed a woman."

"That was the knife attack at Paradise Valley Mall, right? The one he was arrested and sentenced to juvenile detention for?" I asked.

"Yep, that's the one. Bryan told her that the woman looked exactly like his mother from the back. He told Seraphina his mother was deemed unfit to raise him, so they put him in juvenile corrections."

"He's such a manipulator of facts to make it seem like he's the victim, eh? Established the blackout defense early, too. He's gonna use that in our trial," I said. "I just know it."

Marianne said, "Uh-huh, and get this: In Washington he said a woman came into his work with a knife and tried to rob him. He had to spend months in jail, and nobody would believe him. He was just defending himself. They finally believed him, and he was set free."

"Again, such manipulation of facts. He picked that woman up in Washington at a pay phone and tried to stab her in the back like our victims, right?"

"You got it, boss," Marianne said.

William said, "He painted quite the picture of his mother to Seraphina. Bryan said his mother said she wished he was never born. His mother wouldn't let him cry and said men don't cry. His mother hit his head on a concrete wall and came at him with a knife."

Marianne chimed in and said, "And get this about knives, boss! He told Seraphina he was uncomfortable around knives. She said if anyone picked up a knife around him, he would quickly tell them to put it down. He would tell them he had a bad experience with knives with his mother and the woman in Washington."

"Unbelievable! Especially seeing what he did to Angela and Melanie. What a master manipulator!" I said. "She say anything about any porn or deviant behavior?"

William said, "The only porn she could remember was girls in bikinis posted on walls and a few on his computer. Nothing major."

"What did she tell you about his relationship with Randy?" I said.

"Randy was like an uncle to him, and they were really good friends. Randy would give monetary gifts and pay for lots of things for Bryan and his daughter," Marianne said.

"Did she think he took advantage of Randy?" I said.

"Not really. The way Bryan portrayed it to her was that he had been dealt a bad hand in life and was open to people wanting to help him. He deserved that," William said.

"Seraphina and Bryan broke up when and why?" I asked.

"Seraphina said Bryan asked her to marry him multiple times. She said no and then changed her mind. She didn't want to hurt him, but there were too many issues between them. They were very different. She ended up moving out. He begged her not to leave and cried. That was in the middle of 2008."

"What did she think when she found out about our arrest?" I asked.

"She was surprised. She never thought Bryan would do something like that," William said.

"Methinks, as Richard would say, she was lucky," I said. "Lucky to be alive."

"Agreed, and methinks she really felt sorry for him and felt bad for his daughter. However, that was because of how he laid out his past," William said.

"You mean his past as a victim? And one who was afraid of knives?" I asked.

"Indeed," William said.

"Thank you both. It's been a long day. Go home and get some rest. I'll go over Marilyn's interview after we get the baby to sleep tonight," I said.

The house was quiet. The baby had fallen fast asleep, as had Karyn. I was tired, too, from the arrest aftermath and sleepless nights as a new father, but I wanted to listen to what Marilyn had to say about Bryan Patrick Miller. Marilyn was the ex-girlfriend after Seraphina but before Tura and Heather. Marianne and William had told me that there was quite a gap between

Seraphina and Marilyn, stretching from 2008 to 2011. I slipped into my office next to the baby's room. I put on my headphones and listened to the audio feed from my laptop.

Marilyn had met Bryan at an Arizona Steampunk Society event in September 2011. They started dating in January 2012. Marilyn was about ten years older than Bryan. Bryan took her to a shooting range with his daughter for their first date.

As with Seraphina from 2006 to 2008, Bryan was living in what we called the house from hell on Mountain View when Marilyn dated him. Bryan told her he didn't let a lot of people come into his house. Marilyn said Bryan's house was a cluttered and tiny house. He had to clear the sofa off for her to sit the first time.

When they were dating, Marilyn and Bryan filmed a local movie together named *Mantecoza*. The movie was about a man who got hit on the head and ended up in a steampunk world. Bryan had one line, and she had none as she was an extra.

Marilyn said they were supposed to go to a birthday party. Bryan had a black cat named Lucyfur. Bryan ignored the cat, but she was a huge cat lover. Before the party, the cat got out. Marilyn wanted to look for Lucyfur, but Bryan didn't want to. He wanted to get to the party. Bryan then told her the cat was in the middle of the street, dead. Marilyn wanted to come over, get the cat out of the street, and bury it, but Bryan refused. She thought this made him angry and maybe caused him to break up with her. Bryan never picked her up for the party, but she saw that he attended via social media. Bryan lied to Marilyn and told her that she wasn't invited. Marilyn later talked to the host, who told her that of course she was invited.

Bryan stopped talking to her. She asked him why he dumped her and said he gave no response and added later that he didn't know. She figured out that Bryan had left her for Tura. Tura had left her husband and college-aged daughters to be with Bryan. Bryan then banned Marilyn from steampunk events and threatened her with an order of protection for alleg-edly stalking him. Tura even threw her out of a mutual book club. Marilyn later heard that Tura left Bryan and returned to her husband.

Marilyn continued and said Bryan was very gentlemanly during their relationship. She saw no anger issues or outbursts. He never mentioned he had a past with blackouts. She felt he was depressed and had money issues. They had sex during their relationship, but there was nothing she considered weird. In fact, she described it as missionary and "vanilla." The only thing that was strange was Bryan had a hard time ejaculating. She did not see him as violent, but she believed him to be a liar. He told her about his mother's abuse. Bryan said he had fought back against his mother as a teenager and ended up in juvenile detention. He did not tell her about the stabbing at Paradise Valley Mall.

Marilyn said Bryan told her his wife was having an affair. He had gone into their house and found her with a coworker of hers. Bryan told her his ex-wife had no contact with his daughter. His ex-wife had remarried her coworker and had kids with him. Bryan mentioned his ex-girlfriend Seraphina. He said he didn't like her coming over from time to time. She and his daughter were close. He had thrown Seraphina out.

My eyes were getting heavy, but I wanted to hear more from Marilyn. She told the detectives Bryan loved to ride bikes in the past, but he had not done so in a long time. He described himself as a motorhead and enjoyed tinkering with cars. Marilyn said she thought the idea of him owning the converted police car was goofy. Bryan liked to collect things. He was espe-cially into *Star Wars* and Hot Wheels cars. He claimed a lot of the stuff in his house was from his mother and from her time in Hawaii. Marilyn said he had an extensive collection of DVDs, CDs, and videos. He especially liked zombie movies.

Marilyn told detectives she also wondered why his nickname was the Duck 13. She didn't know anything about the nickname or its origin. She did know that he referred to his house as the "duck pond" on social media.

Marilyn reiterated that he was not violent but manipulative. She had not seen knives in the house, and the only gun was a Civil War–era gun.

The recording stopped. We had learned so much about Bryan Patrick Miller. There were still a lot of gaps that we would probably never account for unless Bryan himself filled in the details. The ex-girlfriends painted an interesting picture of how they saw Bryan. One thing resonated uniformly: He told them a skewed version of his past and painted himself as the victim.

CHAPTER 29

THE TRIAL

T he state-of-the-art room was newly constructed, with multiple large-screen televisions on the walls to ensure every member of the audience could see the proceedings. The flags of the United States and the State of Arizona hung prominently at the front. The spacious jury box to the left of the public seating area was uncharacteristically empty. A jury trial had been declined by the defense team in a strategic move. In the history of capital murder cases, it was almost unprecedented to have no jury. The fate of the serial killer instead lay solely with the professional and tough female judge who presided at the center of the room. A team of prosecutors sat in two rows to the left. My bulldog detective team member, the self-proclaimed PhD, William, sat next to them. William had since retired, but he was still as friendly and easygoing as the day we met. To their right, a larger group of defense attorneys huddled. And there he was: the killer who would finally face justice. Bryan Patrick Miller, the self-proclaimed Zombie Hunter, was nestled meekly between them.

I mused at the man who seemed to enjoy hiding behind masks. The media had made the photo of him wearing his Zombie Hunter mask infamous, but Bryan was, of course, not wearing it. A court would never allow for that kind of nonsense. However, he was wearing a light blue surgical-type mask. He would continue to mask his emotions. Richard the profiler loved to talk about how serial killers like Bundy and BTK liked to blend into normal society with false lives and masks of a sort. Bryan was no different.

It was October 2022. More than seven agonizing years had passed since the arrest in January 2015. Tiresome motion after tiresome motion had been made by defense. Additionally, the COVID-19 pandemic had stalled judicial activities for the greater part of the previous two years. The right to a fair trial was paramount, but the legal maneuvering was nauseating. The families needed deserved justice. It was time.

The group assembled to put Bryan Patrick Miller on trial was solid and impressive. Looking at each member individually and knowing that collectively, they had well over a hundred years of trial experience, I knew he would get a fair and impartial trial.

At the center of it all sat Judge Suzanne Cohen. Judge Cohen had served honorably for twelve years as a top-notch and decorated prosecutor for the Maricopa County Attorney's Office. She gained notoriety when she successfully prosecuted the infamous "Baseline Killer," Mark Goudeau, in a capital murder case. It was noted as one of the worst sexual assault and serial murder cases in the State of Arizona. Goudeau savagely murdered nine victims and committed over ninety felonies in the Phoenix area from August 2005 to June 2006. The Baseline Killer was sentenced to death nine times and given over 1,600 years in the Arizona prison system. He currently sits on death row. Prior to her appointment at the Superior Court, Judge Cohen was the bureau chief of the General Trial Group and Family Violence Group. She also was a formidable homicide prosecutor. Before her service in Arizona, Judge Cohen worked in California as a deputy district attorney for two years. She had a stellar background, which would serve her well in this quirky and ultra-challenging capital murder trial.

She had developed a reputation among her peers, defense attorneys, judges, and the general public for presenting cases with massive attention to detail. She was never known to engage in tricks or drama in the courtroom, which served her well and fit with her character.

Judge Cohen looked the part of a prestigious Superior Court judge with her lean middle-aged face and black-rimmed eyeglasses. Her shoulder-length auburn hair was parted neatly in the center and was often curly. I noted during the trial that she had an affable and often witty demeanor with all parties. However, she could definitely be stern when she needed to be, and she had complete control over her courtroom at all times. This would not turn into a media circus like other cases in the recent past.

The prosecutors were led by a seasoned veteran named Vince Imbordino. Vince had longer, slicked-back grayish-white hair complemented by a full beard and mustache. He wore eyeglasses, which accentuated his superior intellect, and was tall and very lean. Vince was soft-spoken and had a Southern accent. He had a very easygoing nature, but he was feared in court by unprepared defense attorneys. He could be tough as nails.

Vince had been a dogged prosecutor for many decades. In fact, a number of the retired homicide detectives I kept in touch with spoke about Vince working with them back in the day. He had developed a solid reputation, which was strengthened with the successful prosecution of the "Serial Shooter" capital case. In that case, two deranged men, Samuel Dieteman and Dale Hausner, committed multiple drive-by shootings and arsons in Phoenix between May 2005 and August 2006. When it was all over, they were deemed responsible for eight murders and over twenty-nine shootings. My team member, Clark, had been the lead investigator on that case and worked closely with Vince.

Vince was joined by an equally tough prosecutor named Elizabeth Reamer on this case. Elizabeth brought over fifteen years of experience to the table and had a solid reputation as well. There were other talented prosecutors who assisted, but Vince and Elizabeth led the charge.

The defense team seemed much larger than the prosecution and led by RJ Parker and Denise Dees. RJ had been an attorney for well over a decade. RJ had thick and wavy coal-black hair and was clean-shaven throughout the trial. RJ was shorter than Vince, but he spoke eloquently and forcefully to make his presence known. He was exceptionally friendly with all in the courtroom, including hardnosed detectives on the other side like William and me. Denise was an experienced defense attorney and spoke directly and succinctly during the trial. Although not as extroverted as RJ, she complemented him well on the team. The well-spoken brunette had straight black hair to her mid-back and mild highlights. Her rounder face was adorned with fashionable eyeglasses.

The prosecution's strategy was to cover the murders in enough depth to establish the crimes and then articulate clearly to Judge Cohen that Bryan Patrick Miller was an absolute sexual sadist who desired nothing more than to sexually assault, kill, and mutilate these young women. They set out to disprove Bryan's defense that he was insane during the heinous murders and rather knew exactly what he was doing. Further, they wanted to show he had clearly planned the murders. Bryan had brought the knife and bodysuit with him, and it was completely premeditated beyond a reasonable doubt. They even pointed to the step-by-step plan written by Bryan and turned over to police by his mother when he was in juvenile detention. Bryan outlined his desire to kidnap, sexually assault, and dismember a woman. The first canal murder, that of Angela Brosso, was much like the plan.

The prosecution phase lasted for three or four weeks. They called William and Clark to testify to their roles as well as the original crime scene detective. The scene detective laid out the crimes and the scenes. Angela's boyfriend at the time, Joe Krakowiecki, testified, as did Melanie's mother. They discussed the evidence and the fact that Bryan was an exact match to the sperm found at both crime scenes and inside both victims. Bryan's ex-wife, Amy, also testified to his violent acts in their sex life. Prosecutors were unable to discuss the related Brandy Myers murder case because of a pre-trial ruling that Bryan's involvement was never proven and may prejudice the proceedings.

The defense strategy had been modified in July 2021. It originally had been to plead not guilty; it had been changed to not guilty because of insanity. They wanted to show that their client, Bryan Patrick Miller, couldn't remember killing these women and effectively blacked out during them. They sought to show through experts he suffered a myriad of disorders, such as autism, anxiety, depression, and PTSD. They also wanted to solidify a proposed psychological theory that Bryan had a dissociative trauma state. During the murders, he transitioned from what they called his normal state to this so-called trauma state, which effectively caused blackouts and lack of memory. Above all, the defense team wanted to demonstrate to the court that Bryan's mother, Ellen, had caused these disorders and made him the monster he was alleged to be. RJ and Denise's job was to not get Bryan set free but rather keep him off death row.

The defense phase lasted for months upon months. One expert somehow produced one of the longest PowerPoints created in the history of PowerPoints to deep dive into Bryan's trauma state versus normal state and his psychological hardwiring. The attorneys brought in witnesses to state Bryan was severely physically and emotionally abused by his mother. They expounded on how he was exposed to and forced to watch pornography at a young age by her. Further, they alleged his mother acted out sexually in front of him. In effect, even though his mother was deceased and couldn't respond to the allegations, she was vicariously responsible for these acts, not Bryan. Otherwise, Bryan was a quiet and shy man, not to mention a loving father with many friends. The defense went so far as to bring in his knife attack of a woman at Paradise Valley Mall when he was sixteen years old. They suggested it wasn't like him, and he snapped out of it after stabbing her. Normal Bryan could not control trauma Bryan.

After the defense rested, the prosecutors presented experienced experts like Dr. James Seward, a published and revered forensic psychologist and neuropsychologist, to refute the statements of the defense experts. They collectively opined Bryan knew exactly what he was doing and was a total sexual sadist.

Vince stood at the front of the courtroom and did something clever and powerful: He brought the case back to the victims during his closing statement. He put pictures of both victims on the large screen for the duration of his statements. Melanie's sister summed it up well when she stated that if a person had tuned in to the trial after the first couple of weeks, they might have thought Bryan was the victim. Vince refocused the trial on Angela and Melanie. The *real* victims.

❧

I exchanged looks with William, who was seated with Vince and the prosecutors. Bryan wore a blue surgical mask and was nestled between RJ and Denise. Over six grueling months of legal maneuvering and presentation had passed. It was April 2023, and it was finally time for Judge Cohen to give her verdict. We were both nervous, as I'm sure were Angela's and Melanie's families. We both knew it was a pretty ironclad case, and DNA did not lie. Yet, I wondered if somehow the defense's tactic of muddying of the waters with psychological trauma and normal states, various disorders, and laser focus on Bryan as the poor little boy victim of a terrible childhood would sway Judge Cohen. It did not. She found him guilty on all six counts (first degree murder, kidnapping, and sexual assault for each victim).

The next phase of the trial was the sentencing phase. Judge Cohen would ultimately decide whether Bryan lived or died. More time passed as the defense team paraded witness after witness to describe Bryan as a shy and caring friend and family member with a troubled past. They collectively claimed he was a loving and devoted father. The defense built a case that his life should be spared.

RJ addressed the judge in a final plea for Bryan's life and told her, "Where would Bryan be now if he had a mother who nurtured him, who gave him hugs and showed him affection, who kissed him with love in her heart?"[1] He continued, "Instead of a mother who withheld affection, instead of a mother who treated him like an inmate rather than a child in his own home, always giving him orders?" Further, he told Judge Cohen that her decision was not of legal nature but a "decision of the heart." He described Bryan Miller as broken, adding, "We should not kill broken people . . . we should work to rebuild them." He asked the judge for her mercy and boldly stated, "Remember that mercy, Judge, is not a weakness. It's a strength."

The families had their turn finally. The impact statements were read to the court. I was brought to tears on this day. As an adult, I had cried only one time before. It was when my mother passed away in 2014 during this investigation. Angela's mother, Linda, spoke to the courtroom via an internet feed. She said, "No, it does not get any better with time . . . I keep waiting to wake up from this horrible dream."[2] She continued, "I will never be able to plan her wedding. I will never have grandchildren. The defendant stole her future, her innocence, her life." She added, "The defendant took my reason to live, my reason to laugh, my reason to love."

Melanie's older sister, Jill, spoke to the courtroom via an internet feed also. Jill said, "The absence we feel in our lives never goes away." Jill told the court her sister was inquisitive, energetic, and outspoken. She added, "A beautiful soul who stood up for kids who were being bullied, even if it meant being bullied herself." Jill described the process of waiting on the arrest and waiting on the trial. "The process takes its toll on the victims." She said her family learned things during the trial and was disappointed by certain people's inaction to come forward with information sooner. Jill said, "We call this out because we find ourselves praying for some glimmer of hope, blessing, or positivity that could come from these senseless deaths . . . something to improve our system to prevent future tragedies. If this is so, finally, just finally, our healing process might just begin. We owe it to Angela and Melanie to do better."

Bryan Patrick Miller finally had his chance. We waited for remorse. We waited for accountability. We got nothing of the sort. Instead, Bryan read the following:

> I am not looking for sympathy today. This time is for the family and the friends of the victims. I cannot imagine what pain they have endured for all these years. I want to just say a few words, and I'm really hoping my words do not cause any more hurt than the families are already suffering. I accept the court's decision, and I'm hoping this trial and my convictions have provided some measure of relief for the families . . .
>
> While I cannot change the past, I can work to have a positive impact on others in the future. I want to do whatever I can to help my daughter . . . I was not a perfect father, but I tried my best. I am sorry for the damage this experience has caused her. I miss her. I want to learn more about myself.

It was June 7, 2023. Eight long months had passed, making this trial one of the longest in county history. Judge Cohen had reached her decision as to the death penalty. The courtroom was packed with family, friends, media, curious community members, and government workers. I was nervous once again. I knew either way Bryan would never see the outside world and would spend the rest of his life behind bars. He would never get to harm anyone or live among us. Yet, I had seen those pictures of what he had done to Angela and Melanie, and they spoke volumes. He had not simply killed them, but absolutely mutilated and destroyed them. In my heart, I felt he deserved the same.

Judge Cohen had prepared a twenty-six-page verdict. She carefully read certain portions to the onlookers and to the families listening virtually. The room was beyond quiet. Judge Cohen went through her findings in summary. Bryan Patrick Miller committed the murders when he was only nineteen and twenty years old. She acknowledged that Bryan had been emotionally and sexually abused by his mother, Ellen. The prosecution showed that Bryan still viewed violent pornography up to the point of his arrest. Judge Cohen indicated that Bryan clearly admitted he got aroused by violent acts, but he had been able to subdue it since the murders. Since the murders, Bryan had married, fathered a daughter, divorced, and been involved in other relationships. Defense had convinced her he was a decent father to his daughter. Bryan had found a community with friends who liked him. This was all true and demonstrated, according to the judge. However, when it came to the matter of whether he was insane at the time of the crimes, he had demonstrated clear premeditation. When he concealed evidence and denied involvement to the police, Bryan was aware of the difference between right and wrong. She continued that the question for the court was "if the mitigation is sufficiently substantial to call for leniency."[3] The judge stopped and briefly looked up toward the ceiling. I took this to mean she had consulted in a religious manner with our maker. She said, "The answer is no." She delivered the harshest penalty, the death penalty, for both murders.

I gazed at Bryan during the decision. He did not move or appear to react. He was stoic. The surgical mask was in place, covering a darker mask he wore.

CHAPTER 30
THE UNKNOWN AND THE CONCLUSION

I stared at Bryan often during the court proceedings. I couldn't help myself. I had so many questions. We had studied him under the strongest of mental microscopes, but there was so much more we wanted to know. Not only his answer to who else he slaughtered, but why and how he did what he did at the canal murder scenes. I peered down at the list of questions I carried with me when I went back to the crime scenes early in the investigation. I also had this same list of questions with me during William's interview with Bryan. I now read the worn and crinkled page but substituted in "Bryan" for "the killer":

- Why did Bryan write *WSC* in dark red (blood/marker/ paint?) on tunnel wall? (Melanie's murder)—three places of *WSC*—body, sign, and tunnel wall—major clue?
- Why did Bryan write *Tweety*? What does it mean?
- What is the relevance of the man in the fedora?
- Any meaning to other markings of *KAW*, *Blitz*, or *Little Devil*?
- Why did Bryan take Angela's head and later place it back in the water? Both scenes involved water—why did he deliberately drag Melanie into the water, risking getting caught? Why did he re-dress her in a young girl's swimsuit? what's the fascination? WATER—why, why, why?

- Why did Bryan use/choose areas near tunnels? Graffiti in tunnel with Melanie and re-dress near tunnel; pedestrian tunnel nearby with Angela. Why?
- Why did he cut their clothing with a knife?
- Why did he leave their shoes and socks on?
- Why did Bryan position Angela with her feet to the east? (Possible religious meaning?)
- Why did Bryan carve *WSC* between Melanie's breasts? What does it mean?
- Why did he carve a cross with three dots below the *WSC* on Melanie? Why three dots on a cross—meaning?
- Religious significance of cutting on Angela? Two round holes in lower midsection; transection of body—cut like cross? Religion again?
- Why did Bryan paint/mark a sign near Melanie's scene *93 WSC*?

I yearned for answers in my every-debit-equals-a-credit CPA mind. I had more for him that I had written on the tattered page:

- Did he act alone?
- Did he videotape?
- Did he go to the church with Angela's head?
- What did he do with his bloody clothing?
- What did he do with the bikes and the Walkmans?
- How did he drag their bodies so far? He seemed very scrawny at the time.

I hoped that someday Bryan will reach out to me and give a tell-all interview. *Bundy did, right? And so did Dahmer. Maybe Bryan will follow suit?*

❦

I jumped up and down rhythmically on a trampoline designed for a toddler. A year and a half had passed since we arrested Bryan Patrick Miller. The new infant in my arms cried hysterically from her persistent colicky belly. I could not soothe her or my own nerves, nor could I keep a watchful eye on my two-year-old, who was now fully mobile in the house. Our hyper boxer dog was another whole issue. Convinced exhaustion was an excellent form of torture, I tried my best to stay cool. My wife, Karyn, needed some time away from the house for herself. I realized it, but it absolutely stunk. What I didn't realize at that time was that things were about to get worse. Rumors had floated about a series of detective and sergeant cuts around the department to shore up patrol vacancies. *Surely, they will realize my cold case team has solved twelve to fifteen cold cases per year dating back to two cases from the 1970s? They will realize we just hunted down a serial killer whom everyone presumed was dead? A wretched killer out and about taunting and posing as a zombie hunter in Phoenix? To dismantle a nationally awarded team who had just won the International Association of Chiefs of Police Award for Excellence in Criminal Investigation and the Chief's Unit Award? Surely that's important, right?*

The phone rang. The baby cried louder. The commander, who had no investigative experience and was set to retire in two weeks, coldly informed me I was returning to patrol. Basically, the cold case homicide squad was being dismantled due to a department-wide manpower reallocation. I felt like I had just been sucker-punched. Woozy, I handed the baby to my father, who had come for a visit. *How could this happen? How could they turn their backs on cold case victims and their families? Doesn't anybody care? Or do they just not know what's going on?*

From that day in 2016 forward, I began working on this book. I felt compelled to tell this story of how a talented team came together and never gave up on these women and their families, a story that to me resonates the sheer importance of cold case teams. They may not get immediate results. It might take years. Sometimes, like in the case of Brandy Myers, it may never happen. But they will never stop trying. In May 2020, I was brought back to the Cold Case Homicide team to restore it to what it was in 2016. I got things back on track with another solid group of investigators and retired at the end of my contractual obligation.

❧

So why a book? One could argue that our success was the ultimate record. It is, but I knew there was more to share with the world than the trial and conviction. I hope that this fuller story honors Angela, Melanie, and Brandy. They had their whole lives in front of them and people who loved them, and that was all destroyed for no reason other than to fulfill the selfish fantasy of some wretched monster.

I also wanted to give the original investigators a powerful kudos for working the cases diligently and maintaining excellent files and records. Without the organized files, we would have never been able to hunt and find the Zombie Hunter. And I wanted to emphasize the importance of maintaining a dedicated, talented, and highly functioning squad of cold case homicide detectives and well-funded DNA labs. I also hope this book has illustrated how never giving up, thinking outside the box, consulting with experts, and teamwork can overcome any obstacle in law enforcement, business, and life in general.

Finally, I wanted to apologize to the CPAs out there. I was rather hard on CPAs in this book. I did not mean to offend. Accounting is a worthy, needed, and challenging occupation. It just wasn't for me. I turned my back on the profession, but it is still a part of me. Further, I do believe the skills of a CPA greatly assisted me in my law enforcement career and particularly this investigation.

TABLE OF ABBREVIATIONS

ACTIC	Arizona Counter Terrorism Information Center
AE	Anger-excitation
AR	Anger-retaliatory
CODIS	Combined DNA Index System
CPA	Certified Public Accountant
DOC	Department of Corrections
DPS	Department of Public Safety
FI	Field Interview
IT	Information Technology
LT	Lieutenant
MCAO	Maricopa County Attorney's Office
ME	Medical Examiner
NCIC	National Crime Information Center
NCIS	Naval Criminal Investigative Service
PA	Power-assertive
PD	Police department
PR	Power-reassurance
SAU	Special Assignments Unit
SRP	Salt River Project

IMAGE CREDITS

ACKNOWLEDGMENTS

- My parents, Barb and Sam, my wife, Karyn, my in-laws, Carol and Clay Crawford, and extended family for the many insights, guidance, and encouragement during this lengthy investigation and the writing of this book.
- My good friend, Mike Tissaw, for listening to me about this case every day on trips to the gym. Your unwavering support was appreciated.
- My college buddy and lifelong friend, Dave McClintic, for his insight into the possible international connection and encouragement during the investigation and aftermath.
- My agent, Lindsey Smith, for believing in me and placing me with a phenomenal publisher.
- My initial editor, Karin Cather, for her insight.
- My writing coach and editor, Chad Rhoad, for patiently teaching me how to write more effectively and efficiently. You are remarkable, Chad!
- My book proposal contributor/writer, Tim Vandehey, for his phenomenal expertise. Tim was a vital contributor to the publishing process.
- My headshot photographers, Tyler Johnson and Spenser Lee at Small Giants Marketing Agency, for their professionalism.

- Retired Detective Bill Stuebe for his mentorship in getting me started in cold cases upon my transfer in 2008 and helping develop policies and review templates.

- Secretary Marge Mawhinney, aka the Colonel, for providing invaluable insight into the murders and unwavering support.

- The following phenomenal leaders for positively impacting my cold case team during not only this investigation but my overall tenure: Dave Albertson, Bryan Chapman, Ed DeCastro, Dave Faulkner, Joe Klima, Joe Knott, Gabe Lopez, Sandra Renteria, and Joe Tomory.

- The original investigator and case agent, Russ Davis, and scene agent, Mike Meislish, supported by the massive team that helped them during the aftermath of these murders, including the Arizona Department of Public Safety crime laboratory, the Phoenix PD crime laboratory, and responding CSI personnel. Without their tireless and diligent work on the front end, these cases could never have been successfully resolved.

- The Cold Case team as written in the aforementioned chapters: JJ Alberta, Mark Armistead, Kelley Merwin, Marianne Ramirez, Dominick "Dom" Roestenberg, William Schira, and Clark Schwartzkopf, plus Phoenix PD crime lab personnel Stephanie Bond and Matt Seabert, and crime analyst Marivic Brotherton.

- The Cold Case Missing Persons team assist on this case of Stu Somershoe and Melissa Pulver (formerly Lutch) for their massive help during the arrest aftermath.

- The Cold Case team assist on this case for their hard work during our investigation and during the arrest aftermath: JJ Cleary, Patty Fimbres, Barry Giesemann, David Hadad, Jay

Hovland, Jerry Hatcher, Josephine Jenkins, Jesse Jimenez, April Lopez, Hugo Lopez, Kirt Messick, Erin Lanning, Don Newcomer, Ken Pollock, Mike Polombo, Jeremy Rosenthal, Dave Saflar, Bob Weigler, and Lois Weiss.

- The Cold Case prosecution team for their years of hard work and dedication in getting ultimate justice for the victims and their families: Jeff Colbert, Vince Imbordino, Elizabeth Reamer, Bob Shutts, Katherine Staab, and Juli Warzynski.

- The Vidocq Society, its leaders William Fleisher and Ed Gaughan, and especially profiler Richard Walter, for guiding us on these investigations and providing insightful input.

- Forensic genealogist Dr. Colleen Fitzpatrick, for introducing us to the very powerful crime-fighting tool of forensic genetic genealogy.

- The numerous Fugitive Apprehension, Special Assignments, and Repeat Offender Program officers who tenaciously arrested, conducted surveillance, detained and served warrants on multiple leads in this case.

- The Phoenix Air Unit pilots who tirelessly flew my team members to numerous destinations to obtain interviews and DNA from leads.

- Attorney Dale Norris for helping my cold case team on a pro bono basis start the Arizona Cold Case Investigators Association and bring the Vidocq Society to Phoenix for training.

- SilentWitness.org for their unvwavering support of solving cold cases and partnership with our cold case team.

- My apologies if I have overlooked or forgotten to specifically name someone. So many people positively impacted these cases.

NOTES

Chapter 5: The FBI Profiles

1   T. F. Salp, "Unknown Subject; Angela Marie Brosso—Victim (Deceased)," Federal Bureau of Investigation, February 22, 1993.

2   M. Safarik, "Unknown Subject; Melanie Bernas—Victim (Deceased)," Federal Bureau of Investigation, December 12, 1995.

Chapter 10: The Connections and the Cyberstalker

1   "Lemuel Prion," Murderpedia, the Encyclopedia of Murderers, 2014, http://murderpedia.org/male.P/p/prion-lemuel.htm.

2   P. Angel, "Mother Comes to New Mexico to Look for Daughter, Answers," *Las Cruces Sun News*, October 2, 1992.

3   Andie Adams and Dave Summers, "Incriminating DNA Found Inside Cold Case Victim: Warrant," NBC 7 San Diego, October 31, 2014, https://www.nbcsandiego.com/news/local/incriminating-dna-found -inside-cold-case-vicitm-claire-hough-warrant-kevin-brown-ronald -tatro/62306.

4   C. Vaughn, "El Dorado–Sutter Decapitation Murders," True Crime California, November 15, 2012, http://www.truecrimecalifornia.com /?p=439. This article is no longer available online.

5   "Nearly 22-Year-Old Case Still Elusive," *Daily Courier*, March 19, 2009, https://www.dcourier.com/news/nearly-22-year-old-case-still -elusive-article_14ba7653-f169-539f-bdc0-ede7725a2c87.html.

6   "Swedish Nanny Murder," Celebrate Boston, n.d., http://www .celebrateboston.com/crime/swedish-nanny-murder.htm.

7   "Joan Archer," Pima County Sheriff's Department, November 22, 2010, http://www.pimasheriff.org/bulletins/bulletin-details/?ref _cID=1268&bID=0&dd-asID=3.

8   Pima County Sheriff's Department. (2010, August 26). Crystal
Matis. Retrieved from http://www.pimasheriff.org/bulletins
/bulletin-details/?ref_cID=1268&bID=0&dd-asID=3

Chapter 11: The Modern Day Sherlock Holmes
1   Ed Pilkington, "Vidocq Society—the Murder Club," *The Guardian*,
March 3, 2011, https://www.theguardian.com/world/2011/mar/03
/vidocq-society-cold-case-murders.

Chapter 13: The Vietnam Vet and the Eyes
1   Associated Press, "Convict Seeking Freedom Blames Vietnam for
Slaying," *New York Times*, September 13, 1981.

Chapter 14: The Grim Sleeper and the Pilot
1   L. Sher and N. Karlinsky, "New Technique of Using Family's DNA
Led Police to 'Grim Sleeper' Suspect," ABC News, July 8, 2010,
https://abcnews.go.com/Nightline/familys-dna-led-police-grim
-sleeper-serial-killer/story?id=11116381.

Chapter 29: The Trial
1   Lane Sainty, "Canal Killings Trial: Bryan Miller's Attorney Asks
for Mercy As Sentencing Nears," *Arizona Republic*, May 24, 2023,
https://www.azcentral.com/story/news/local/phoenix/2023/05/24
/canal-killings-trial-bryan-miller-attorney-mercy-death-
penalty/70238137007/
2   Colleen Sikora, "'Canal Killer' Victims' Family Members Share
Statements in Court," 12news.com, April 18, 2023, https://www
.12news.com/article/news/crime/impact-statements-given-by-families
-of-canal-killer-victims/75-ea8b395a-259e-4719-9b7f-ed67503dfa61.
3   Michael Kiefer, "Trying a Death-Penalty Case Without a Jury Is
Practically Unheard of in Arizona," *AZ Mirror*, June 15, 2023, https
://azmirror.com/2023/06/15/trying-a-death-penalty-case-without-a
-jury-is-practically-unheard-of-in-arizona.